The Inspired Dream

PLATE 1
Pansy Napangati
Papunya/NT
Winpirri rockhole 1987
Synthetic polymer paint on canvas
139 x 140cm
Warlpiri Language Group

Winpirri is an outcrop with waterholes, west of Papunya. The central roundel is the site at Winpirri. Surrounding this site is a large claypan which is depicted in the central panel. This design represents the cracked surface of the claypan once the water has soaked away after the rain. Forming the claypan's boundaries are two, vertical wavy lines, which represent spun hair string. This is human hair string, which is spun for decorative ceremonial items. The 'U' shapes are two women of the Dreamtime, who passed through Winpirri on a long journey to the east coast of Queensland, all the way to the salt water of the Pacific Ocean. The women's digging sticks and coolamons (oblong shapes) are also depicted.

The Inspired Dream
Life as art in Aboriginal Australia

Edited by
Margie K.C. West

Presented by
the Museums and
Art Galleries of
the Northern Territory

in association with the
Queensland Art Gallery

Queensland Art Gallery
South Bank
South Brisbane
Queensland

PO Box 3686
South Brisbane Qld 4101
Australia

Typeset in
10½/13pt Veljovic Book

Organising Curator
Margie K.C. West

Curatorial Assistant
Catherine Robertson

Production Assistants
Roland Dyrting
Steven Klose
Jens Pedersen
Cynthia Coyne

Exhibition Officers
Joe Devilee
Michael James

Designer
Michael Ward

Typographer
Steve Landon

Photographer
Ray Fulton

Style Editor
Di Furness

Copyright Clearance
Aboriginal Artists' Agency
Artarmon Galleries

Photographic credits
Plate numbers shown in italic

Margie K.C. West
2, 3, 10, 18, 20, 22, 23, 24
George Chaloupka *4, 5, 6, 9*
Paul Taçon *7*
Dr Luke Taylor *11*
Françoise Dussart *15*

National Library of Australia Cataloguing-in-Publication data:

The Inspired Dream.

Bibliography.
ISBN 0 7307 0021 6.

[1]. Aboriginal Australian art – Northern Territory – Exhibitions. 2. Northern Territory. Museums and Art Galleries Board – Exhibitions. I. West, Margaret K. C. (Margaret K. Cameron), 1950- . II. Northern Territory. Museums and Art Galleries Board. III. Queensland Art Gallery. IV. Expo 88 (Brisbane, Qld.).

709'.9429'07409943

Contents

Preface

PLATE 2
Clifford Possum Tjapaltjarri painting dots on canvas, Alice Springs.

Aboriginal art in the 1980s continues to excite and extend white Australia's perception of Aboriginal culture and its art forms. It refuses to be defined. Previously designated by outside imposed stereotypes, Aboriginal art has been discovered to be more than x-ray bark paintings and, more recently, more than 'dots and circles.' By expressing and recording social laws, titles to land, historical events and major religious stories, the art exists in many forms. Although most of the pieces contributing to *The Inspired Dream – Life as art in Aboriginal Australia* are from the visual arts, they represent the tip of an iceberg of performing arts which continues in ceremonies today. It is a dynamic living culture. Even within the area of public visual art, Aboriginal art is changing in response to outside influences. For example, one of the major art movements in the last twenty years in Australia has been the 'Western Desert' school which started in Papunya with the introduction of new media. It has awakened white eyes to a large area of 'undiscovered' artists and art forms.

Current interest in Aboriginal art and its commercial spin-offs has had positive and negative effects. The need for art pieces has led to the 'discovery', artistically, of previously unappreciated Aboriginal groups. So it has broadened the base of the outside world's contact with Aboriginal cultural expression. At the same time however, there is the danger that the pressure to produce is putting a strain on the creative process. Inspiration through dreams and interpretations of religious stories cannot be forced. The responsibility put upon artists to rationalise this balance between commercial demand and their own creativity is immense. However, Aboriginal artists have risen to this challenge and have surprised, delighted and moved the 'art' and 'public' domains by replying to the pressures that have been placed on them and the Aboriginal world in general.

John Mundine
Arts adviser
Ramingining Arts and Crafts
Arnhem Land

Foreword

PLATE 3
Johnny Bulun Bulun painting a design on bark, Maningrida.

The Queensland Art Gallery is delighted to present the exhibition *The Inspired Dream – Life as art in Aboriginal Australia* throughout the entire period of World Expo '88. It is also timely to present a large audience with an exhibition which so graphically reveals the contrasts with white Australia's European-based cultural traditions.

Drawn from the specialised collection of the Museums and Art Galleries of the Northern Territory in Darwin, the exhibition is certainly specific in representing regional areas and communities, but it also helps to depict Aboriginal Australia as a whole. *The Inspired Dream* clearly shows the continuity of cultural patterns from early times to the present day. Aboriginal art is a shared cultural experience and a vital aspect of day to day living. It is an art which has been carried down through the generations as a way of communicating beliefs, information and ideas.

This exhibition is not a short-lived or celebratory gesture, for the Gallery has made a commitment to develop further its Northern Australian Aboriginal and Islander Collection and to give it greater presence within the development and the display of the permanent Collection.

The Gallery gratefully acknowledges the support and co-operation of the Museums and Art Galleries of the Northern Territory in lending material for this exhibition and special appreciation is extended to the Director, Dr Colin Jack-Hinton, and the exhibition's Curator, Ms Margie West.

Doug Hall
Director
Queensland Art Gallery

Introduction

The antiquity of the Aboriginal people's occupation of Australia is still not definitely known. Tantalizing pieces of evidence, a few human remains and copious numbers of stone tools and associated food and other camp debris, have indicated an Aboriginal presence in Australia for around 40,000 years. It is possible that people migrated from south-east Asia to the Australian continent much earlier than this. However, positive evidence to support this is yet to be found.

The durable remains of these first Australians, in particular their stone tools, indicate a conservative history, with only two major tool technologies occurring during this vast time scale. On the other hand, something of the cultural diversity and complexity of these early inhabitants – their aspirations, fears, beliefs, aspects of their environment and their social structure – is hinted at by the wealth of images which are found on rock surfaces throughout the continent.

Antiquity and continuity of Aboriginal art

The more durable engravings which are cut into the rock's skin are believed to represent some of the earliest examples of man's creative expression. Ochre images trapped behind glassy layers of silica in some areas may also be of a comparable age. Unfortunately, due to the lack of suitable techniques for dating images on rock, much of the dating is relative, based on such things as the succession of superimposed styles and the subjects depicted. Contributor George Chaloupka discusses this in his article on the chronology of rock painting in western Arnhem Land. The art of this region presents an historical depth to Aboriginal man's artistic expression which may go back to the very early period of his occupation, continuing through to the present to remain as an important aspect of contemporary Aboriginal life. The continuing significance of this art tradition is an aspect further explored by Paul Taçon in his article on western Arnhem Land rock art.

The changes and the recent continuity of stylistic traditions evident in this rock art highlights the dynamism of Aboriginal culture, which has managed to sustain the tremendous impact brought about by the arrival of new settlers on their land. In western Arnhem Land for example, people's contact with these early European and Asian migrants, and subsequent decimation through disease, reduced numbers by an alarming degree. The survivors drifted to settlements or missions often far from their clan lands and associated rock art sites. So by the early 1900s rock art gradually ceased to be produced, and painting on pieces of bark began to supersede it as a medium of expression. With encouragement from a few anthropologists and missionaries in the regions of Arnhem Land, the practice of bark painting spread, so that by the 1950s communities from Bathurst Island to Yirrkala were producing portable barks for sale. Prior to this, the main form of bark painting practised by many groups was the decoration of their stringy-bark, wet-weather shelters, to pass the time as well as to instruct young initiates in the stylistic and mythological traditions of their group.

To most people, bark painting has become synonymous with Aboriginal art. However, painting onto bark is only one facet of what constitutes Aboriginal creative expression. Fortunately the persistence of what could be termed neo-traditional Aboriginal lifestyles in the northern and central regions of Australia, has provided the outside world with a greater understanding of the range of artistic expression and its function and significance for its producers.

It is particularly the diverse and visually complex art of the groups living within the Northern Territory that has given us these insights, and in fact provides the focus for *The Inspired Dream* exhibition and this publication. Even in the exhibition, only the more durable aspects of Aboriginal art, such as paintings and carvings, are presented, omitting much of the ephemeral media such as body paintings, elaborate head ornaments, ground designs, sand sculptures and the songs, dances and oral traditions which are usually associated with their creation.

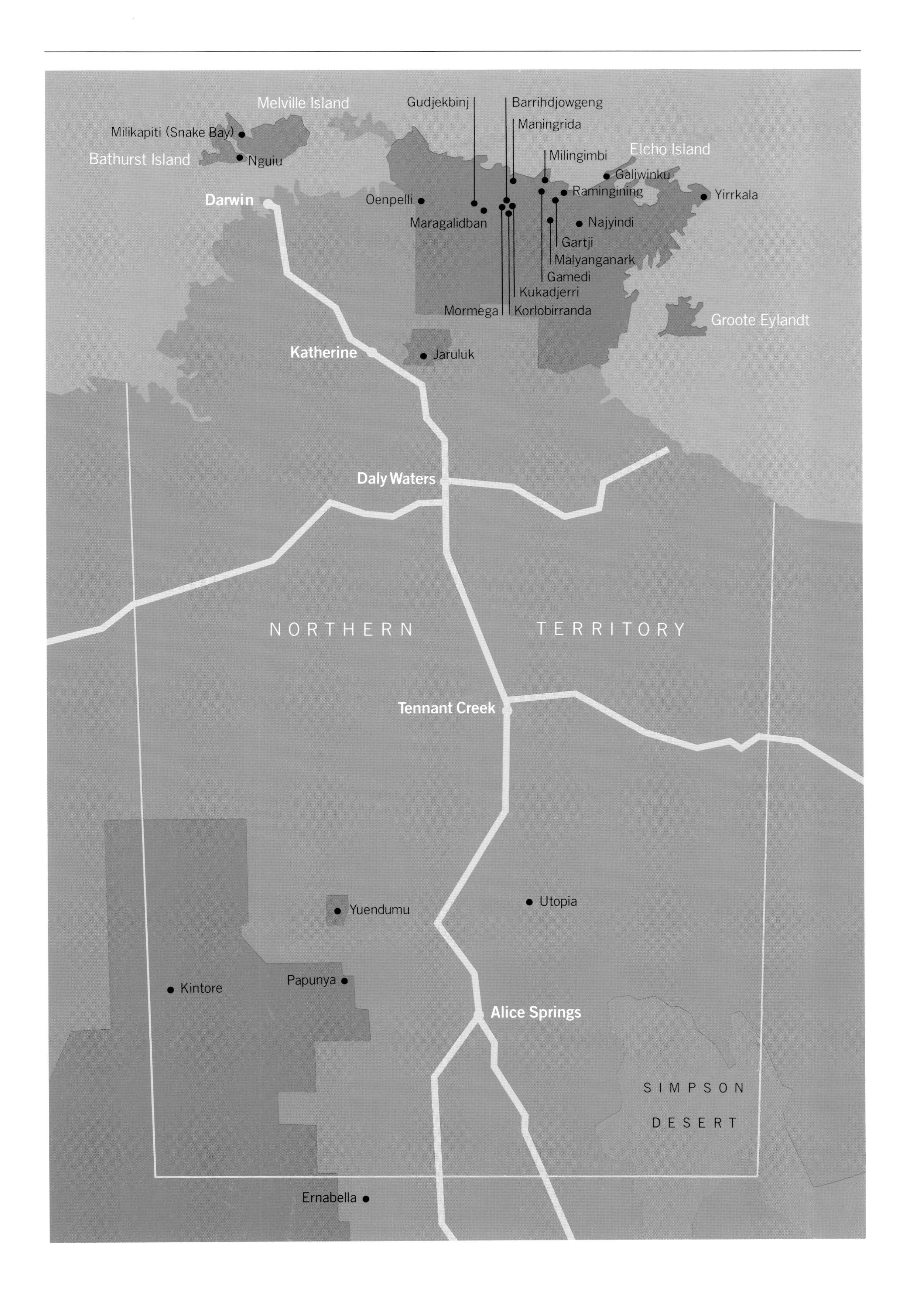

Melville Island
Milikapiti (Snake Bay)
Bathurst Island
Nguiu
Darwin
Gudjekbinj
Barrihdjowgeng
Maningrida
Milingimbi
Elcho Island
Galiwinku
Ramingining
Yirrkala
Oenpelli
Maragalidban
Najyindi
Gartji
Malyanganark
Gamedi
Kukadjerri
Mormega
Korlobirranda
Groote Eylandt
Katherine
Jaruluk
Daly Waters
NORTHERN
TERRITORY
Tennant Creek
Yuendumu
Utopia
Kintore
Papunya
Alice Springs
SIMPSON
DESERT
Ernabella

Themes of Aboriginal art

In these small-scale societies where all aspects of life are much more integrated than our own, artists illustrate the wide range of experience available to them. This is reflected in the arrangement of the exhibited works into categories based on the themes of Aboriginal people's relationship to their natural environment and to their spiritual world.

As hunters and gatherers, Aboriginal people depended upon their extensive knowledge of the environment and subsistence strategies for their very survival. They devised elaborate taxonomic classifications for the plants and animals around them and knew exactly where and when to find resources for their food, medicines, stimulants and for the production of their art and items of material culture. The animals, plants and natural phenomena of their environment are also included in the social order by being given totemic relationships with particular groups of people. Many of these species are also regarded as important Ancestral or Creation Beings which are the focus of important rituals. Because of this, people's relationship to their environment was not simply economic, but it was also social and religious. This interrelationship between all aspects of life is also stressed by Jon Altman in his article on contemporary art and craft and the economy, and this fact emphasises the difficulty, even for thematic purposes, of separating subjects portrayed in paintings. For even though there are illustrations of everyday subjects, such as hunting and gathering, or animal and plant species of the environment, there is an overlapping between the mundane and religious nature of works, which is influenced by the religious philosophy of the Dreaming.

This religious philosophy lies at the very heart of the Aboriginal social and cultural heritage as it explains the origins of their known world. According to this belief, a variety of Ancestral Beings emerged from the inanimate earth in human or animal form. They travelled the land, created various aspects of the natural world and handed down the social rules and rituals necessary for sustaining life, maintaining order, and transferring knowledge and ownership of the land.

The exploits of these Beings are dramatised in important ceremonies which in turn provide the focus for the most elaborate forms of artistic expression. During these rituals the exploits of certain Ancestral Beings are re-enacted or evoked to release their Ancestral power for the achievement of certain ends. This could be the continued productivity of a particular group of people or plant and animal species, or the guidance of a person's soul to its final resting place. Regional concerns also underscore the particular type of ceremony performed. In the arid desert areas of central Australia, for example, where food and water could sometimes be scarce, ceremonies were principally concerned with the productivity of man and his resources. Rain ceremonies were especially important here. In contrast, groups inhabiting the richer environments of the north were more concerned with death and mortuary rituals. These usually incorporated aspects of initiation and were the most elaborate ceremonies performed. Today these rituals continue to play an important role in the religious life of the people of these regions, where the ideology of the Dreamtime remains as the unifying concept which links the economic, social and religious aspects of life into an articulated whole. In the illustration of this interrelationship, life in Aboriginal society is very much reflected by its art.

Symbolism and meaning

Art is used particularly in ritual contexts to embody and convey complex messages, using a set of symbols which operate like a visual language to convey meaning. It is this symbolic nature of Aboriginal art which is its most important characteristic.

For example, contributor Howard Morphy explains how, in north-eastern Arnhem Land, the geometric designs characteristic of this area can embody a variety of meanings which relate to clan identity, ownership of land and relationships to particular Ancestral Beings and their associated ritual connotations. Similarly, Françoise Dussart talks about the narrative possibilities offered by the set of symbols used to construct designs in the art of central Australia. These circles, lines, arcs and semi-circles can assume a variety of meanings according to the story being told. They can also mean a variety of things simultaneously, thus condensing deeper levels of meaning along with the 'outside' non-sacred ones. While much has been written about the many levels of meaning embodied in the geometric art from north-eastern Arnhem Land and the Western Desert, it is fascinating to discover from Luke Taylor that the art of western Arnhem Land, which is essentially naturalistic, has a similar symbolic function.

The use of symbolism in the varying styles employed by the diverse cultural groups of the Northern Territory emphasises that the true meaning of such paintings often goes deeper than their recognisable physical attributes suggest. Through this visual language artists can condense a lot of information which can be political and social, as well as religious.

The fact that artists derive their inspiration from their religious beliefs in the Dreamtime or Dreaming underlies the theme selected for the exhibition – *The Inspired Dream – Life as art in Aboriginal Australia.* This also has a duality of meaning because the dream is also considered to be the vehicle for artistic invention or innovation. Artists often talk about how they 'dreamt' a particular design or certain way of expressing their traditional repertoire of designs and stories. The 'dream' in such cases is not seen as a means of individual creativity, but rather as a way of tapping directly into the source of Ancestral power, and this legitimates innovation within the accepted limits of stylistic convention. This capacity for change is built into Aboriginal artistic systems and rather than reflecting some sort of loss of cultural purity, as some traditionalists would believe, it is rather a normal response exhibited by any society. There is no such thing as 'traditional' in the sense of some immutable static 'norm.' This is merely a tag used to describe Aboriginal practices as they were recorded at the very earliest period of contact.

Contemporary Aboriginal art

There is no doubt that the sort of outside changes which have impinged upon Aboriginal groups in these northern parts has escalated in past years, particularly through the emphasis on economic self-sufficiency stressed in the current government policy of self-management. Of the 30,000 Aboriginal people living in the Northern Territory today, about 20 per cent produce art and craft for sale. This has generated some significant changes, such as the increased input by women in the plastic and graphic arts and the adoption of new media such as watercolour, acrylic, batik and silkscreening for the production of art works. Modifications of traditional artistic systems have also occurred in some areas, to protect the secret and sacred aspects of the art. For example, in north-eastern Arnhem Land the incorporation of figurative elements along with the geometric clan designs has in effect extended the ways in which artists can portray the various aspects of their Dreamings. Ian Green in his article also discusses how the evolution of contemporary central Australian designs have been achieved by the elaboration of background patterns alongside the traditional set of abstract symbols.

The capacity for change inherent in the symbolic nature of these artistic systems, and the sanctioning of innovation through dreams, has allowed contemporary artists to modify certain aspects of the formal representation of their Dreamings without affecting their intrinsic meaning. For example, a canvas painting of an Ancestral journey from central Australia is still regarded by its author as a powerful representation of Ancestral knowledge and a confirmation of associated claims to country and ritual responsibilities. As several of the authors have stated, the sale of paintings to outsiders today, although motivated in part by the need for money, is seen as a way of extending certain levels of Aboriginal knowledge and political concerns to a wider audience. The appreciation and purchase of such painting, is seen by the artists as a sanctioning of their religious and political reality by non-Aborigines.

There is no doubt that the more sensitive and informative approach to the display and marketing of art works through 'thematic' groups or individual artist's displays, has generated a greater understanding of Aboriginal art in recent years. It is a significant development in cross-cultural appreciation that the more esoteric forms of ritually related art, such as geometric bark painting and desert canvasses, have found a steadily expanding market – a far cry from the days when the most acceptable art to the public at large were the representational landscape paintings from the Hermannsburg School, founded by Albert Namatjira. This is not to diminish the artistic merit of such watercolours. However their eclipse in recent years by works which are regarded as being more 'traditional' in their genesis, reflects a greater willingness to accept the uniqueness of Aboriginal art.

The year in which *The Inspired Dream* exhibition is being staged, apart from being the year of World Expo '88, is also the year of Australia's Bicentenary. This celebration of 200 years of European occupancy in Australia has been seen as inappropriate by many Aboriginal groups, resulting in boycotts and the adoption of the theme, 'we have survived.' In a sense 'survival' is what is reflected in this exhibition of art works from the Northern Territory, which includes images of the very earliest expression of Aboriginal art from the faces of rock shelters to the contemporary pieces in batik, silk-screen or acrylic, as well as on bark. The tradition of western Arnhem Land x-ray painting and central Australian geometric art found in the rock art shelters of these regions and currently being reproduced by contemporary artists, emphasises the considerable antiquity of these stylistic traditions. The continuity of such artistic endeavours, along with the recent incorporation of certain changes, also illustrates the resilience and strength of the Aboriginal people, whose paintings still reflect the fundamental motivating influences which define and set them apart as a distinct cultural group.

MARGIE WEST

Rock art of the Northern Territory

PLATE 4
This rock painting is located in a shelter on the edge of the Simpson Desert in central Australia. It is typical of the geometric art of the region and is still reproduced in body decoration, ground designs and on ritual objects during ceremonies.
No further details were given because of the sacred nature of the design.

Rock art, in the form of rock paintings or rock engravings, is found throughout the world, almost everywhere that suitable rock shelters, or rock formations and surfaces are located. On every continent, from the most northern to the extreme southern latitudes and even on the far-removed islands stretching across the Pacific, man – from the time that he emerged as *Homo sapiens* – began to make visual statements about his physical, social and cultural environment. Artistic creativity became one of his fundamental needs, skills and characteristics. Some of the world's masterpieces, executed on the walls and ceilings of the caves and rock shelters which were his home, bear witness to his early artistic accomplishments. Such painted and engraved images are also found in Australia, where the rock art traditions are rich and varied, and their forms expressed in a wide range of styles and techniques.

The three most extensive Australian rock art complexes are situated in the tropical north. The spectacular Wandjina paintings typify the art of the Kimberleys in Western Australia; the complex and colourful x-ray paintings exemplify the art of the Northern Territory's Arnhem Land; while the large stylised paintings of Ancestral figures and animals represent the art of Queensland's Cape York. The rock art of these three locales documents the cultural complexity and creative achievement of the Aboriginal populations who had lived in this land for 2,000 human generations before the First Fleet sailed into Sydney Harbour. It represents their contribution to mankind's cultural heritage, and is recognised for its aesthetic merits, inventiveness and sophistication.

Northern Territory rock art

The rock art regions of the Northern Territory are situated in the centre of a vast cultural zone which spans the north of the continent from the north-west coast of Western Australia, through the Kimberley region, across Arnhem Land and the Gulf of Carpentaria, to Cape York in the east. It extends from the island and coastal shelters, where it may have been influenced by contact with south-east Asian civilisations, to the very centre of the continent.

The body of rock art within the boundaries of the Northern Territory was recorded from the very early period of exploration, beginning with Matthew Flinders' expedition in 1803. Since then thousands of additional rock art sites have been recorded and many still await discovery. The majority of these sites are located in the 'Top End' – the Arnhem Land Plateau region – and in the ranges of the Victoria River District. There are also numerous sites in the intermediate locales, on Groote Eylandt and other coastal islands, in the Gulf of Carpentaria region, and in the Centre (Plate 4).

Here a variety of techniques are used in the creation of rock art. Vivid ochre pigments of red and yellow ochre, white clays and black charcoal or manganese, are used for the colourful images present in the rock shelters. These comprise stencils of sprayed pigment, imprints of hands or objects, drawings in dry pigment and paintings in wet pigment. In some instances rock painting has been deliberately combined with engraving techniques, where the image is either abraded, incised, scratched, pecked or formed by a combination of two or more techniques.

Only a few simple engravings have, however, been recorded in the Arnhem Land Plateau region. This technique is more common further west and inland from Katherine, especially in the Victoria River District. Further inland, engravings become the major expressive art of the Centre, where old and weathered engravings and pecked rock surfaces burnished by the desert winds, bespeak their antiquity.

At several locales, pellets of beeswax have been pressed onto the rock to form simple and complex abstract designs, as well as human, anthropoid and animal figures. This unusual technique appears to be restricted to the Arnhem Land Plateau region.

Rock art of the Arnhem Land Plateau

The largest and best known complex of Northern Territory rock art is in the Arnhem Land Plateau – a vast sandstone island rising above the adjacent lowlands, some 250 kilometres east of Darwin. A spectacular escarpment cut by deep gorges and valleys with numerous waterfalls and waterholes, forms the plateau's western and northern margins. This area, drained by the South East Alligator Rivers and their tributaries, was referred to in the past as the Alligator River region or as western Arnhem Land. At present it is the Kakadu National Park. Here 120 rock art sites have been recorded within an area of 5 square kilometres, and this is not an unusual concentration. Fortunately the wealth of rock art and other sites of significance documented within its boundaries are assured of distinction due to the World Heritage listing of Kakadu National Park.

The Aboriginal groups whose traditional lands lie within this area, exploited not only its rich riverine environment but also that of the adjoining flood plains, freshwater swamps, lowlands and pockets of savannah. The availability of water, a relative abundance of resources, as well as suitable rock shelters along the escarpment and its valleys, made the area attractive for settlement and exploitation.

The geology of the plateau is dominated by two rock types, stable orthoquartzites and the less stable, weathering quartz sandstone. The major art sites with well-preserved paintings are found mainly in the shelters of orthoquartzitic rock, which provides a smooth, stable surface for painting. Paintings on quartz sandstones are considerably weathered and, in instances where the rock surface itself is disintegrating, only traces of the original designs now remain.

Although absolute dating of the earliest rock paintings of this region is as yet not available, the circumstantial evidence suggests that the painted images found in its shelters may represent the oldest, and the most significant expression of human creativity. This is an important proposal, because previously it was believed that the Ice Age rock paintings from Spain and France represented the beginnings of man's artistic activity. The supporting evidence for the antiquity of this rock art is based on the analysis of data gained from nearly 2,000 rock art sites found in the region. In the first step of this study, the individual styles, representing the varying artistic traditions that followed each other throughout millennia, were identified and defined. In many instances, images in a number of styles were painted over each other on the walls of the one shelter. The order in which they were superimposed was therefore used to develop their chronological sequence. This was followed by a detailed analysis of the content of each style for it became obvious that certain subjects were present in one or more styles but absent in others. The reasons for this were sought in the archaeological, climatological, geomorphological, zoological and botanical evidence, and in historical records. Theoutcome of the study was a temporal rock art sequence of four main periods: **pre-estuarine, estuarine, freshwater** and **contact.**

The pre-estuarine period

It is proposed that the **pre-estuarine** period, consisting of a number of rock art styles, commenced during the peak of the last Ice Age some 18,000 years ago, and may even predate it. At that time the sea was 150 metres lower than at present. A land bridge connected Australia to Papua New Guinea, and continental shelves extended to the vicinity of the Indonesian Islands. Archaeological deposits document the presence of Aboriginal people within this region during the **pre-estuarine** period. Used pieces of ochre found throughout the deposits date back 25,000 years. A 19,000 year old red ochre impregnated grindstone shows that during this time ochres were prepared into pigments, and an analysis of silica skins, formed over painted surfaces, indicates that the images beneath are more than 10,000 years old.

The following sequence of styles was identified during this period:

Hand prints, grass prints and imprints of thrown objects
Large naturalistic figures, animals and human beings
Dynamic figures
Post-dynamic figures
Simple figures with boomerangs
Yam figures

The earliest images of this period are hand prints, grass prints and imprints of thrown objects. Hand prints were made by placing the hand into a wet pigment and then pressing it against a rock surface. Grass prints and imprints of thrown objects are thought to be contemporaneous with hand prints. They were immersed in the pigment and struck against the rock face. These simple images were followed by accomplished paintings of animals which were frequently portrayed larger than life and depicted in a naturalistic manner. The majority of species represented were macropods, echidnas, emus and freshwater crocodiles. The rock paintings of this period also depict animals that are either extinct or no longer present in the Northern Territory – for instance the *thylacine* (or Tasmanian tiger) which has been extinct on the Australian mainland for some 4,000 years. The Tasmanian devil, also depicted in painted shelters, survived in the north until 3,000 years ago, as was confirmed by excavating and dating his remains. Perhaps the most exciting discovery in this region's rock art was a painting of what is thought to be *Palorchestes,* a large browsing marsupial tapir, representing extinct Australian megafaunal species. This find complemented the previously recorded painting of *Zaglossus,* a long-beaked echidna. As these two animals were contemporaneous, and as their remains found in caves throughout Australia were dated to the last Ice Age, rock paintings documenting their presence in the Arnhem Land Plateau are perhaps of similar antiquity – more than 18,000 years old.

Along with paintings representing the animal species are depictions of human beings, mainly men. These too were occasionally executed larger than life-size, with the heads shown in profile detailing their features; their extremities, hands and feet, were similarly elaborated. These two distinguishing aspects have suggested the description for this style as *large naturalistic figures.* Humans and animals were, in most instances, represented as single images. The art of composition was to commence with the style that followed.

The *dynamic* figures style consists of small, exquisitely executed drawings of human beings, anthropomorphs, animals and composite beings. They were sketched onto the rock surfaces in expressive movements, and arranged into narrative compositions depicting people's economic and socio-cultural activities (Plate 5). The typical male figure wears an elaborate head-dress, a hair belt from which hang one or two pubic fringes of varying size and shape, and decorative necklaces, pendants, armlets, tassels and leg ornaments. Their weapons consist of barbed, single-piece wooden spears, a number of boomerangs and clubs, hafted stone axes and throwing sticks. The female, depicted without any bodily decoration or apparel, is usually portrayed carrying digging sticks, dillybags and occasionally spears, fire sticks or a stone axe. Animal-headed beings were frequently depicted as participating with human beings in a number of activities. Animals are portrayed in detail and, with the exception of the megafaunal species, are of the same species as those depicted in the previous style. The fish, represented for the first time, are of the freshwater species. Some of the human and anthropoid beings, as well as the animals and their tracks depicted in this style, are surrounded by dashes, while similar marks emanate from their mouths. It is suggested that these signs depict aspects of the artist's sensory experience such as sound, smell, force, anxiety and, in the case of animal tracks, their freshness. The artist of the dynamic figures style was an accomplished draughtsman and an innovator who, in his complex compositions, preceded similar achievements elsewhere by many thousands of years.

In the following style the human figure, though at first closely resembling the dynamic figures, became progressively stylised, losing much of its previous animation, to appear finally as frontal, and static. Because of this development these representations are termed the *post-dynamic figures.* Later, human beings became further schematised, to become in time, one-line thick, stick-like figures named *simple figures with boomerangs.* The term boomerang was used to

distinguish these figures from other simple stick-like figures executed in subsequent periods when this weapon was no longer used. In this style the hunter figure, although greatly abstracted, continued to be portrayed wearing a head-dress, pubic fringe and associated with weapons previously used.

The last style of this **pre-estuarine** period, that of *yam figures,* was expressed in paintings of naturalistic symbolism, when images of yams were transposed into human, animal and mythic forms. This style developed over time from simple representations of yam tubers with their vines into a phytomorph, a plant-like being, and finally into man, associated with weapons and implements. The characteristics of the yam were also imposed over that of a turtle, flying-fox, birds, representations of the Rainbow Snake and a number of animal beings. As there were no representations of yams in the previous rock art styles, this focus on a plant subject suggests its importance to the artist, perhaps as a food source. The change from the naturalism and stylisation of the previous styles to the symbolism expressed in the yam figures reflects change in the artist's psychological environment. This, and perhaps the previous changes in stylistic expressions, may have been due to the effects of the then rising sea level on regional populations, as the loss of large areas of land required adaptation and a conciliatory philosophy.

It is possible that the rapidly rising sea level may have also led to the inception of the Rainbow Snake belief. In the majority of northern myths this Rainbow Snake Being is associated with the rain and floods. In the coastal variations of the myth, the Rainbow Snake emerges from the sea and swallows and drowns people. The Rainbow Snake is represented in rock art in a number of awesome forms during the subsequent periods. The myths of the Rainbow Snake are recounted, its sacred sites are respected and this Being continues to play its major role in the ritual of various other regions of the Northern Territory today. The conception of this Being in such an early style, its depiction in all the following styles, and its appearance on contemporary bark paintings, documents the longest continuing religious belief in the world.

The estuarine period

The **estuarine** period commenced between 7,000 and 9,000 years ago when the sea rose to approximately its present level. At that time, lower valleys and trenches of rivers and creeks filled with salt water and estuarine clays, creating a broad salt marsh environment adjacent to the plateau and its outliers. The incoming tides on the East Alligator River reached into the escarpment introducing new species of animals. This major environmental change is reflected in the region's rock art. Paintings of the giant perch, or barramundi (*Lates calcarifer*), mullet (*Liza alata*), lesser salmon catfish (*Arius leptaspis*) and the estuarine crocodile (*Crocodylus porosus*) first appear on the walls of rock shelters to become, in time, the dominant subjects. The new tool technologies developed for hunting are also depicted – the hunters are portrayed with multi-pronged fish spears and spearthrowers. Boomerangs ceased to be represented as they were no longer used in hunting or fighting, although they appear in later compositions used as music-sticks during ritual. The environmental change also caused shifts in the habitat of the animals previously occupying the pre-estuarine plains. Some were forced to move further inland while others became extinct, such as the *thylacine,* which was then no longer represented in the rock art styles of this period.

PLATE 5
On this rock, in Kakadu National Park, a man is depicted spearing an emu with a barbed spear. This style has been called the dynamic figures style and is represented by small, exquisitely painted figures with an array of body ornaments and weapons.

PLATE 6 *(over)*
This rock painting depicts Darwin wharf and several boats, from the turn of the century. The Aboriginal artist has carried the exact images of the boats in his mind and reproduced them in this shelter hundreds of miles away in Kakadu National Park.

The rising sea levels and the accompanying increase in rainfall culminated in prolonged wet seasons, with their electrical storms and cyclones. This gave rise to the myth of *Namarrgon,* the Lightning Man, who is frequently depicted in rock art. A band encircling his body symbolises the lightning, while the stone axes which he holds in his hands, and other axes attached to different parts of his body, were used to split the clouds and cause thunder.

After the naturalistic phase, which marked the commencement of the **estuarine** period, the intellectual realism of the descriptive and decorative *x-ray* styles became the major art expression of this and the following periods, although other forms of expression were also used. In the descriptive x-ray style, the artist depicted not only the subject's external form, but also its internal features. Animals are shown in their dominant recognisable aspect, generally in profile, with their internal organs and bone structure. In the continuing elaboration of this style, some artists ceased depicting the anatomical details of internal organs and subdivided the animal's body into patterned forms hence the term decorative x-ray style.

The freshwater period

Another major environmental change occurred when the freshwater billabongs and paperbark swamps developed over the previously saline plains, some 1,500 years ago. The annually flooded wetlands became then a major habitat of important waterfowl species such as the pied goose (*Anseranus semipalmata*). Pied geese, other bird species, as well as new plant species, were also depicted in rock art, replacing all the previous styles and subjects. Rock paintings of pied geese and of their hunters (who would carry a goose wing fan and short goose spears made of light reed shafts and tipped with a sliver of hardwood) typify this period. Paperbark rafts poled by women into the wetlands to collect goose eggs in season, and waterlilies which they gathered later in the year, are also represented in the rock paintings. It is possible that the aerophone – the *didjeridu* – was then invented or introduced because, in compositions where this instrument was used, some participants are depicted carrying a goose wing fan. Environmentally this period has persisted into the present.

The contact period

The last major rock art period of the Arnhem Land Plateau is that of **contact.** Paintings of the **contact** period vary from the previous two styles only in subject matter, as the stylistic conventions and painting techniques then developed continued to be used. This period commenced several hundred years ago with the first visits by the Macassan fishermen from what is today the Indonesian Island of Sulawesi. They came to the northern coast to exploit the shallow seas for bêche-de-mer (or trepang) favoured by Chinese as a culinary delicacy with aphrodisiac properties. Their boats – the prahus – are portrayed in rock paintings, as are some of the weapons and other objects of their material culture. The Macassans were only seasonal visitors, arriving with the north-west monsoon at the beginning of the wet season and leaving for home with the south-easterly wind of the following dry season. On some of these voyages they were accompanied by Aborigines who, on their return, depicted the strange things they had seen overseas on the walls of their rock shelters.

Most of the early European contact was also limited to the coastline – along the Cobourg Peninsula and extending in later years to Darwin. Fort Wellington was occupied for two years between 1827 and 1829 while the Victoria Settlement at Port Essington was established in 1838 and abandoned in 1849. The history of European settlement in the north could be reconstructed from the region's rock paintings. The first images are of boats and ships which sailed along the coast. Some of the paintings of boats are accompanied by depictions of guns and exotic animals, such as the buffalo, which were brought to provide a reliable meat supply for the early settlements, but escaped or were released to overrun the land. In the 1890s the buffalo shooters moved into the Alligator Rivers region to exploit their numbers, shooting them for their hide. They were to become, with their horses, rifles and skinning knives, a favourite subject in a number of rock shelters. There are also paintings depicting the passage of early explorers, buffalo shooters pursuing their prey, a painting of a model-T Ford, a biplane, a twin-engined plane and portraits of missionaries. Paintings representing the Chinese working on the Pine Creek railway, and the Darwin wharf of the 1890s, also show the Aborigines of this region to be keen observers (Plate 6).

The internally painted and decorated hand stencils and beeswax designs belong to this period as, in many instances, they are associated with **contact** subjects. The majority of sorcery paintings are also associated with this period. They are perhaps a direct consequence of anxiety, stress and introduced sickness, such as the documented epidemics of influenza, measles and leprosy which affected perhaps the majority of the groups living in this region.

The last rock paintings executed in the *x-ray* style were painted in 1964, and the last known paintings in this region were of a white silhouette of an agile wallaby and a goanna, painted in 1972. The rock art of the Arnhem Land Plateau region, as reflected in the chronological sequence of its art styles, represents not only the world's longest continuing tradition of this art form, but it also documents, in its detailed narrative compositions, the longest record of human endeavour.

GEORGE CHALOUPKA

Contemporary Aboriginal interpretations of western Arnhem Land rock paintings

There are many ways of responding to a work of art. Yet our knowledge and understanding of a particular piece can be enhanced considerably by placing the work in time and space, in a cultural perspective, and in the larger artistic traditions of the region from where it originated. Though this may be done from an archaeological, art-historical, environmental, ethnographic or even psychoanalytical point of view, the best approach is one that combines all of these.

Previous studies of prehistoric art, such as rock paintings, have often been limited to descriptions of its form. Little attention was paid to what indigenous peoples had to say about their own artistic heritage (often the art was used to test, support or explain theories popular at that time). By ignoring or diminishing this vital perspective, our understanding of the expressive nature of art has suffered.

In many regions of the world it is obviously too late to obtain an informed, 'inside' look at particular forms of prehistoric art because the people now living in the region are totally divorced or removed from it. However, certain ancient artistic traditions have survived up to very recent times or they continue, in a slightly altered form, in new, contemporary media. Also, some forms of prehistoric art are still used today in a symbolic context and because the designs still have meaning, they are highly valued by the indigenous peoples who are descendants of those original creators. This is particularly true of the western Arnhem Land region of Australia's Northern Territory where many Aboriginal elders related to rock artists of the recent past retain knowledge about the production, function and meaning of rock art.

The rock painting tradition

Western Arnhem Land, including the World Heritage Kakadu National Park, is one of the most concentrated regions in the world for rock art. In Kakadu alone it is estimated that there are at least 5,000 individual rock art sites and these vary in age from less than a few years to possibly 18,000 years or more.

The numbers of paintings at particular sites vary tremendously. Some sites contain only one motif, such as a hand stencil or stick figure, while others contain up to a few hundred individual paintings. Occasionally they may be arranged in elaborate compositions or scenes, but they frequently consist entirely of individual works. Often numerous layers of painting are evident and, in some cases, up to a dozen overlapping works may be identified.

It is this overlapping or superimpositioning that helps us identify successive styles or forms of painting and gives us a clue as to its sequence or chronology, as well as its time scale (see Chaloupka's contribution in this volume). The majority of art sites with superimpositioning also served as shelters and living

PLATE 7
Bobby Nganjmirra stands in front of a rock painting of x-ray style kangaroos. Injuluk, Oenpelli, western Arnhem Land.

areas for Aboriginal people. At many sites evidence of this may be seen in the form of stone flakes or tools, burnt animal bones or more elaborate artefacts. A number of sites from different parts of the region have been excavated and these archaeological investigations have revealed that Aboriginal people have lived in the area for at least 25,000 years.

The most recent period of rock painting was one of great diversity and elaboration and differs from earlier periods in terms of subject matter, form, use of colour and symbolic content. It is this art that is still very important to Aboriginal people even though some of the paintings in this style were done hundreds of years ago. This recent style has been labelled 'x-ray' by previous scholars because paintings which illustrated internal features tended to dominate. However, it is now emerging that x-ray paintings are part of a much larger artistic system. Because of this, one should more properly talk about an 'x-ray period' rather than a 'style' or about an 'x-ray motif' that has been added to some paintings, in varying degrees but not to others. This is more in keeping with the Aboriginal perspective of the art and also allows one, more precisely, to define and understand the nature of recent rock painting in the region.

Most x-ray rock art appears to have been produced over the past 1,500 to 3,000 years when freshwater environmental conditions, similar to those of today, developed and persisted in the greater part of the Kakadu landscape. Some very simple monochromatic red x-ray forms, however, may be as old as 8,000 years of age and some aspect of internal detail can be found in rare instances in earlier art styles as well. The most recent x-ray rock paintings were produced in the early 1960s by the Aboriginal artist Najombolmi and many of the paintings found throughout Kakadu are attributed to him.

Some of the others were made by cousins, brothers, fathers, uncles or grandfathers of Aboriginal elders living in Kakadu or adjacent areas today and they followed the stylistic conventions of their predecessors closely. Internal anatomical features illustrated by Najombolmi and other artists include the backbone, long-bones, the heart, lungs (or air sac in fish), liver, kidneys and other organs; the diaphragm, fat, flesh, muscle, body cavities; the alimentary canal or digestive tract or some part of it; dividing lines separating chambers, types of tissue, organs or skeletal structure; body fluids, such as breast milk in women; and, occasionally, optic nerves. Even European objects, such as guns and boats, sometimes had their internal features highlighted. Red, yellow, white and purple are the predominant colours but orange, pink, black and an introduced blue were used occasionally. The x-ray tradition continues on barks and many early bark painters may have also painted in rock shelters (Plate 7).

Along with the x-ray paintings of humans, animals and mythical beings, numerous solid or stroke in-fill subjects were created. These differ from their x-ray counterparts only in terms of internal detail and otherwise have a similar form. Aboriginal people argue that they depict 'dead' or 'cooked' beings while x-ray paintings depict living creatures. For them, the two forms are part of a larger system of artistic expression, and paintings with solid or stroke in-fill are not incomplete x-ray paintings. The x-ray art, however, has greater potential for expressing meaning, due to its multi-layered form and structure.

Various forms of stick figures were also drawn or painted in shelters and these vary from static, straightforward poses to energetic, elaborate postures suggesting movement and action. Around Ubirr, Oenpelli and the north-eastern edge of Kakadu many large scenes of stick figures can be found arranged in postures suggestive of warfare. Often the stick figures hold spears or spearthrowers and sometimes volleys of spears are depicted overhead. Many figures have open mouths suggesting cries of victory or anguish and most have male genitalia prominently featured. Limited skirmishes are known to have taken place in the area in the past and Aboriginal elders remark that they portray fights over land or women. Other stick figures were composed into hunting, ceremonial or domestic scenes or were painted as solitary, static entities. Most static stick figures lack sexual characteristics and appear 'casual' and non-specific.

Generally, stick figures appear to be more commemorative and historic in quality than x-ray or solid in-fill paintings, in that they refer to specific events and have more-or-less set interpretations. This is true of most of the smaller, detailed figures but some of the larger stick figures (usually over 30 centimetres) with exaggerated, attenuated limbs are said to be depictions of Spiritual Beings, such as the *mimi,* which inhabit the area. As well as this, ancient, pre-x-ray paintings of 'dynamic' stick figures or other subjects are said to have been done by the *mimi* before Aborigines lived in the area. (The *mimi* originally taught Aborigines how to paint.)

Hundreds of hand, hand-and-arm and artefact stencils cover shelter walls and ceilings as well. Occasionally a foot stencil or a stencilled outline of an animal's body part can also be found. Aborigines state that most stencils were made in order to record a visit to a site and to remember particular individuals. Stencils were made by men, women and children, whereas most other forms of painting were done exclusively by men. Some stencils have been painted with clan designs and x-ray features, such as finger bones, to produce striking images to honour the memory of particular individuals.

A variety of sacred symbols, or *mardayin* designs, were painted in some shelters as well as various geometric shapes, lines or patterns. Some stick figures, abstract designs or animal forms were also formed out of pressed beeswax. Sometimes beeswax was added to a painting composed of pigment to create a three-dimensional effect.

The arrival of Asians and Europeans in the north of Australia has been recorded in the art in great detail. Ships at anchor or ready to sail, smaller prahus (Indonesian boats), steamers and row boats, an aeroplane and men on horseback, document the passage of outsiders through western Arnhem Land.

With the arrival of foreigners, there was a heavy toll on Aborigines in terms of disease, loss of land and loss of culture. Ian Keen, for instance, estimates that 'the Alligator Rivers Aborigines and their neighbours to the west had been reduced to about 3 per cent of the population at the time of contact' (1980:171). Some of this is reflected in the art of the period, with sorcery paintings being the most dramatic response. As sorcery was thought to have caused disease and misfortune it was often expressed or avenged through painting.

Although there was great upheaval in western Arnhem Land in the early period of the twentieth century, this did not result in a major reorientation in the form and style of artistic expression. Change was merely incorporated into it and earlier conventions have persisted until recent years. As well, much of the inherent meaning and importance of the paintings has remained unaltered, so that for many Aboriginal elders the rock art expresses a great deal about both contemporary and traditional life and belief.

Art as an expression of life

Aboriginal elders remark that most paintings done in shelters that were used as living areas were of things thought to be good, such as fish, other food animals or women. Dangerous subjects, such as evil spirits, sorcery paintings or venomous snakes, were painted in out-of-the-way places so as not to bring harm to one's kin group. The most frequent subject found in x-ray art is that of fish, as they were considered to be of both symbolic and economic importance. Fish are an easily available, staple food resource posing little threat to human life. Furthermore they are related to the rainbow and the Rainbow Snake, through the colours of their skins. They are also symbolic of the beginning of life. Snakes, on the other hand, can represent food (harmless snakes or pythons) or deadly enemies (brown snakes) and have to be treated with caution. They too, are related to the rainbow and the Rainbow Snake but, because of their power, aggressiveness, swallowing and regurgitating capabilities, they are more symbolic of the end or birth of life. As a consequence, the only depictions of snakes in living shelters are of harmless snakes or pythons. Other creatures sought after for food were also painted in shelters. Macropods, consisting of various species of walleroo and wallaby, echidnas, turtles, goannas, possums, magpie geese and other species abound in the art. Fish, however, reign supreme. A recent study

PLATE 8
Crusoe Guningbal
Barrihdjowgeng/NT
Mimi spirits c.1970
Ochre on wood
186.2 x 8 x 7.2cm
76.2 x 6 x 5cm
Kunwinjku Language Group
Narrangolo Clan

Mimi *spirits live amongst the rocks in the sandstone escarpment region of western Arnhem Land. They are tall and thin so they can slip easily between the cracks in the rocks. They are said to be extremely shy, so very few Aboriginal people claim to have seen them. Crusoe was the first artist to carve* mimis *in this non-ceremonial form.*

has revealed that they comprise over 62 per cent of more than 3,000 x-ray paintings examined (Taçon 1986, 1987a, 1987b).

A further 12 per cent of the paintings were found to be of human beings and two-thirds were of women. X-ray humans differ from x-ray animals in that internal organs, such as the heart, liver, kidneys or intestinal tract, are not illustrated. Long-bones are usually intimated by thin lines and backbones often consist of only two thin parallel lines that are occasionally segmented. Generally, there seems to have been less attention paid to internal detail in x-ray depictions of humans. In fact, many paintings of humans have had more attention paid to external detail, such as the illustration of body painting or breast girdles.

As hunter-gathers and warriors, dealing frequently with death, Aboriginals realised that, physiologically, humans do not differ that radically from other animals. The reason for the difference in the paintings lies, instead, within the realm of spiritual belief. Evil *Namorodo* spirits, found throughout the countryside, guide the spirits of the recently departed away from their bodies. At night they often appear in the sky in the form of a shooting star, while during the day they sometimes take on a guise of a white-breasted sea eagle or some other large, predatory bird. These spirits live off the heart, intestines and other internal organs of the sick and dying for up to a week before death. If one were to depict human internal features in paintings on shelter walls, then one might attract these spirits to the camp and bring harm to the group. This dichotomy between animal and human x-ray paintings subtly, but very expressively, illustrates an aspect of belief that would be irretrievable without 'inside' information (Plate 9).

Most paintings of animals, including fish, were done after the hunt and not before. Very few were related to hunting magic. Occasionally, however, someone might retouch or add features to a pre-existing painting if they had been unsuccessful at bringing back a catch. Animal paintings also could be used in a variety of other ways – to teach, explain, illustrate or pass on aspects of traditional belief and practice.

Visual expression throughout Arnhem Land is closely related to myth and ritual, and according to Forge the three appear 'to be completely interlocked and interdependent.' All are equally powerful as mediums of symbolic communication, and all three are 'different ways of expressing aspects of the same thing in words, in actions, and visually, none of them being complete without the other, and none of them being the entire expression on its own.' (Forge, 1971:293)

At one large site with a few hundred paintings this relationship became especially evident, as many were found to illustrate simultaneously more than one event, myth, practice or belief. A group of different animals with x-ray features, for instance, was said to represent

animals caught by people who had previously camped there; but the animals were also grouped to illustrate a certain creation myth.

At another level, the internal features and markings told how one should cut up and cook certain animals and then how the meat should be distributed. The features could also be used as a 'map' with some of the anatomical parts representing geographical features to instruct youths about places that were good for hunting. Many other practical aspects about hunting and fishing could also be conveyed. Even laws and cultural traditions were explained in this way.

At a much deeper level, some of the paintings were used to convey more secret and sacred information to the initiated. As an expression of metaphysical belief, the art not only aided the discussion of complicated matters, such as notions about life and death and reincarnation, but also increased the level of awareness among those who studied it. With its play between the internal and external, x-ray art is analagous to the 'inside' and 'outside' meanings of art forms and of life itself.

In western Arnhem Land, the visual and oral traditions of passing down knowledge and experience have to be understood as components of a larger form of cultural expression. Today, with accelerating change and the passing away of many knowledgeable elders, art has taken on an increased importance. It has become a vehicle for passing on Aboriginal knowledge, traditions, culture and belief, not only to Aborigines but also to others. As Bill Neidjie of the Bunitj clan has said, the art is like a history book and by studying it one can learn about life and, in the process, about oneself:

> *This one, now, history, history book; good for you. My history, this why I'm telling you. You might as well listen this one. And give you all that feeling good. And think about by yourself. If someone, silly man, that's the one, he's stirring you up, don't listen; you might get in trouble.*
>
> *One day you might sorry. This thing make you sorry, ya know, one day. If you really know, it'll make you sorry. But that silly man, he don't know...*
>
> *But this now history. History good for you, to listen. Think about it by yourself. You might like it... I like 'em this one. This make a man sit up. Give you flavour. Give you feeling, better.*
>
> *You know sometime you get accident, sometime you get killed. You never know, might be snake kill you. Silly man, he go swim now crocodile because he don't think about it. You think about all this history, you look. Think about yourself. That's all.*
>
> *Silly man, no matter good friend, but if no good, well what? --- sometime accident. Same with Aborigine. If you miss all this story, well bad luck; you can't help 'em any more. Telling story more better, good for us.* (Neidjie in Tacon, 1986)

Conclusion

There are many things we can learn from Aboriginal people and their art. One of the most obvious is that particular pieces or forms of art do not always have set meanings or interpretations.

Usually, however, each work encompasses only a set range of symbolic meanings pertinent to the society that produced it. This is true not only of Aboriginal art but also of our own. Our system of art history, regrettably, has been obsessed with finding set, exact and ultimate meanings in art. In the process, we have limited our range of thought and belief and restricted our understanding of reality. Aboriginal art and culture and the system of Aboriginal 'art history' is much more open-ended and allows for individual experience and individual reality in interpretation. It seeks to discover meaning in life, in art and in belief and to answer fundamental questions of existence. In so doing, it opens avenues of understanding and helps one realise the multi-dimensional nature of existence. In reaching a further understanding one 'gets that feeling' and feels better because of it. And as Neidjie has stated, "If no good, I wouldn't tell you about this... you might as well listen this one and give you all that feeling good."

Contemporary interpretations may, of course, differ from those of the artists who created these paintings some fifty, one hundred or one thousand years ago. Because they are shared by a number of people over a large area and are fundamental to the belief system. However, it is likely that they vary only slightly within the parameters of individual experience. The increased importance of rock painting to the remaining Aboriginal elders has occurred as a consequence of the tremendous change in other areas of Aboriginal life but the art was *always* an important vehicle of expression. Today, perhaps, it is more important because of the sense of urgency that rapid change has brought about.

PAUL S.C. TAÇON

PLATE 9 *(opposite)*
An x-ray painting of human beings and fish are illustrated in this painting from the Kakadu National Park region.

New life for the Dreaming:

Continuity and change in western Arnhem Land bark paintings

For the Aborigines of western Arnhem Land, bark painting represents a means of educating both an art-buying public and the younger generation of Aboriginal children into a distinctive way of looking at the world. Bark paintings present images of the original creators, the Dreamtime Ancestral Beings, which moulded the landscape, created humans and instituted all their cultural practices. The creation of bark paintings is a vitally important way of maintaining traditional religious belief in the power of these Beings. While the Ancestors are indirectly revealed in such things as the contours of landscape or the energy of ceremonial performance, bark paintings display the form of these Beings with an immediacy that is matched by no other medium. Bark paintings bring the viewer face to face with the Dreaming; the power of the figure is exposed through the aesthetic force and intellectual complexity of the image. If we are sensitive to their purpose, we can see how the artists have used the market for bark paintings and public exhibitions of their work as a means of bringing a wider audience into direct contact with this alternative reality.

The setting

Artists in western Arnhem Land are concentrated in the Aboriginal towns of Oenpelli, Maningrida, Jaruluk (Beswick), Bamyili and Katherine and many live in small bush camps called outstations in the region bounded by these larger centres. The languages spoken are Kunwinjku, Dangbon and Rembarrnga.

The movement towards living in small bush camps represents an attempt to regain control of traditional lands after a period of considerable interruption to the traditional settlement pattern. Outstation life is characterised by a strong interest in hunting and gathering combined with an increased interest in ceremonies. Bark paintings reflect the liveliness of both these concerns to contemporary artists (Plate 10). Outstation living differs from the traditional lifestyle in that it also involves the use of such modern aids as motor vehicles, two-way radios and shotguns, as well as regular visits by mobile shops operating from the towns.

PLATE 10
Johnny Bulun Bulun painting a design on bark, Maningrida.

The marketing of bark paintings is organised by art advisers who work in the local centres and visit the small communities regularly. Advisers are responsible for the purchase of works and for arranging their resale to southern states. They may also host visiting collectors, organise exhibitions or arrange for the artists to travel to attend the openings of major exhibitions. While the art advisers are employed by local Aboriginal co-operatives and work to ensure the highest possible monetary returns for the artists, they are also involved in ensuring the quality control of paintings and in communicating the desires of the market back to the artists.

To date, the interaction between western Arnhem Land painters and the wider Australian market has not resulted in significant changes in the form of paintings. Contemporary bark paintings diverge very little from the forms exhibited in the traditional rock art of the region and in the earliest collections of paintings on the walls of bark shelters. There has been a move towards the depiction of more important ceremonial subjects and the incorporation of ceremonial painting styles. This move came about as the artists perceived that the outside world was interested in their 'Dreaming' or major religious subjects. The development of the market for bark paintings has been greatly influenced by people who had a keen interest in the religious preoccupations of Aborigines, and art has been promoted because it provides a window to these beliefs. Most art advisers have been sensitive to the complexity of Aboriginal religion and have encouraged artists to portray their most important subjects.

Traditionally, in western Arnhem Land, the most popular type of public art consisted of paintings of common food animals. Paintings of food animals, in the x-ray style, abound in the rock shelters spread throughout the western Arnhem Land region. Today there is a market demand for such works and artists will often paint figures in this way on smaller bark paintings intended for the tourist market. To satisfy the demand for more important ceremonial figures, artists now paint larger barks showing Ancestral Beings in human or animal form. These paintings are distinguished by the use of elaborate cross-hatching techniques to in-fill the outline of the figure. Naturalistic x-ray details may be absent or reduced to a highly geometric form. The way the figures of Ancestral Beings are in-filled are borrowed from ceremonial paintings worn on the body or painted on ceremonial boards. This stylistic evolution in western Arnhem Land bark painting suggests certain similarities with eastern Arnhem Land art, where body paintings and bark paintings are closely allied. It is possible that early collectors encouraged this parallel development in the bark paintings of the two religions. However, western Arnhem Land artists use ceremonial patterns in a distinctive way.

In eastern Arnhem Land, artists apply cross-hatching in regular sequences of colour which are meaningful in terms of the mythology of the clan. Cross-hatching patterns are intimately linked with design components that identify the subject's clan affiliations. By contrast, western Arnhem Land artists do not consider cross-hatching in bark painting to be meaningful in the same way. Though cross-hatching does communicate the Ancestral origin of the subjects, artists are free to be innovative. The manipulation of cross-hatching patterns to suggest striking visual activity is an aesthetic effect artists consider appropriate in the representation of the Ancestral power of the Being. This power is likened to the lightning which accompanies wet season storms, and in paintings of some Beings, cross-hatching is used to represent these thunderbolts. Senior artists may experiment with different kinds of patterns by varying the colour sequences or the angle of cross-hatching to create visually exciting contrasts. In some cases the artists settle on particular in-fill techniques that identify their individual works. The same techniques can be adopted by younger artists apprenticed to the older men and thus a wider group or school can be distinguished by the way they share certain stylistic traits.

The system

While western Arnhem Land paintings have their innovative aspects, the production of paintings does follow a general pattern which is understood by senior men and women. Different types of western Arnhem Land bark paintings are related in a systematic way. These relationships help to create the symbolic qualities of the paintings.

Paintings of food animals or mayt

In paintings of ordinary animals, or *mayt* (the Kunwinjku word for animal), western Arnhem Land artists are restricted to representing the features that identify the species in a clear and unambiguous way. Aborigines recognise very fine differences in the body shape of particular animals, and the artists are careful to ensure that a specific type of animal can be easily read from the image. For example, characteristic features such as the lump on the head of the magpie goose or the spatulate beak of the spoonbill bird are represented in a naturalistic way. The best artists strive to achieve a harmony between the elegant portrayal of the animal body shape, the inclusion of its identifying features and the rhythms created by the interior in-fill of the figure. Aborigines from this region also gain considerable aesthetic satisfaction from accurate portrayals of the characteristic movements of certain species – the sinuous twists of the crocodile, or the kangaroo that swivels its head to watch a hunter.

Paintings of animals frequently include hunting scenes or scenes of butchering and cooking. A common format consists of a large animal figure in association with a thin, stick-like human figure clutching a spear and spearthrower. These thin human figure shapes represent the *mimi* spirits which are said to inhabit the caves of the western Arnhem Land escarpment. Paintings of these figures are thought to be faithful renditions of the long, tall, body forms of the spirits who slip in amongst the rock fissures by day and roam the country at night. *Mimi* spirits are often shown performing other activities such as dancing or playing music in much the same way as contemporary humans. The *mimi* are not considered powerful like Ancestral Beings, but they are said to have taught humans how to perform some ceremonies and how to hunt and cook in the correct way. One common type of painting shows the *mimi* cutting up game. Contemporary hunters follow relatively strict rules for cutting and apportioning game – rules which were instituted by the *mimi*. Paintings of animals with naturalistic representations of internal body parts, such as the heart, lungs, liver, stomach and intestines, are explicitly related to the customary division of game. Frequently artists paint dissected animal figures, and occasionally paintings show single body parts. Because such body parts have a characteristic shape, it is usually possible to tell which species they belong to.

Paintings of Ancestral Beings or D̲jang

Paintings of more important Ancestral subjects or *Djang* (the Kunwinjku word for Creator Being) can sometimes be distinguished by the way their transforming potential is represented. Such paintings provide an outlet for considerable creativity amongst western Arnhem Land artists. The Ancestral Beings are said to have been able to undergo transformations from animal to human shapes, and sometimes artists paint figures undergoing this transformation. Recognisable features of certain species are mixed with human forms. The Ancestral Beings are also said to have been transformed into features of landscape or sacred wooden objects, and sometimes these alternative metamorphoses are also represented. These more complex paintings highlight the way Aborigines from this region see a relationship between all the manifestations of the Ancestor. Many different kinds of objects, as well as humans and animals, are considered to be linked, because they are part of the same essential spiritual essence – the original Ancestral Being which created them all. Often, certain objects or features of the landscape are described as the transformed parts of the Ancestor's original body. Myths often relate to how the Ancestral Beings were cut into pieces and how the pieces transformed into other objects. Such imagery is related to the more mundane world of the butchering of animals for food, but the symbolism of the scene relates to many other realms of experience.

The representation of transforming body shapes is most apparent in paintings of Yingarna, the major creator figure and the original Rainbow Serpent and of her mythical son, Ngalyod. Yingarna and Ngalyod are often painted with a body form that suggests the amalgamation of body parts from many different species. Yingarna can be painted with the identifying body features of a crocodile, kangaroo, snake, barramundi and waterlily; this identifies the major transformations of this Being. Ngalyod is often shown to be more like a snake, but any of the species mentioned above, and many more besides, could also be incorporated. In such paintings, the artists have created a major all-embracing symbol. In ceremonies of the region, initiates learn that Yingarna created all subsequent Ancestral Beings and was 'mother to them all,' and that all the Ancestral species emerged from a hole speared in her side. Sometimes this 'birth' is explicitly represented in bark paintings. By visually combining characteristics from many species, western Arnhem Land artists have created a figure with a body form which reflects all that is known of this creation myth. The paintings help younger people to understand the qualities of these Creator Beings.

Today, the social life of western Arnhem Land people is in a considerable state of flux. Individuals can move widely over the region and choose to live in lands situated well away from their own clan territories. Clan-based ceremonies are not as important today as the much larger ceremonies, such as Kunabibi, which draw participants from all over the region. It is these ceremonies which stress the importance of Yingarna as the original creator of the Ancestors of all clans. With increased mobility, and the expanding popularity of these major ceremonies, Aborigines of the region are developing a sense of wider unity. The comparatively recent paintings which show Yingarna as an amalgam of many other Ancestral species augment this development. Senior artists, as ritually knowledgeable men, are in a position to facilitate social and ritual change through the creation of symbols which show the connections between people that exist over and above clan distinctions.

X-ray paintings

Another important feature of western Arnhem Land bark painting is the elaboration of the x-ray technique of in-filling animal and human figures. Artists vary the type of x-ray in-fill to suggest different meanings for otherwise similar paintings.

The most common style of x-ray in-fill consists of relatively naturalistic motifs representing the internal organs and bones. It is used in paintings of ordinary animals and shows the important edible portions. Western Arnhem Land Aborigines are familiar with the meanings of the relatively limited set of motifs which are used to represent particular organs.

Predominantly skeletal x-ray in-fill associates the figure with death and decay and the more enduring spiritual aspect of a figure. Western Arnhem Land people speak of the souls of the dead having the form of skeletons, and the use of skeletal x-ray identifies the spiritual form of a figure. For the Aborigines of

PLATE 11
David Milaybuma is a well known artist from the Maningrida region in central Arnhem Land.

western Arnhem Land, death does not represent the total extinction of a being. People believe that beings have two spirits, a ghost or profane spirit and a more sacred soul. At death, the ghost is believed to stay near the body until purification ceremonies are held to chase this spirit away to infrequently visited jungle areas. The sacred soul, on the other hand, is closely associated with an individual's clan identity and, at death, ceremonies are performed to ensure the return of this soul to the sacred sites of the clan. These souls can then be reborn as children belonging to the clan. The meaning of bark paintings showing skeletal subject matter is continuous with the meaning of skeletal body paintings worn in the old Wubarr and Mardayin ceremonies and in contemporary Lorrkon and Mamurrng ceremonies. These ceremonies have obvious mortuary components, with additional themes of fertility and the recycling of human souls.

Another type of x-ray in-fill consists of a combination of geometric components, such as grids of dotted dividing lines, motifs like circles and triangles, and multi-coloured cross-hatching. This type of in-fill is called *rarrk* and it is reserved for the depictions of Ancestral Beings. It is interpreted as showing the internal organs of the Ancestral Beings, as well as features of the landscape. Thus, in western Arnhem Land, artists' figurative paintings present the paradox of figures which show features of landscape within them. The geometric x-ray in-fill relates directly to the *rarrk* designs used in Mardayin ceremony. These designs are associated with a number of levels of meaning, primarily, the representation of important features of landscape in the clan lands of the person wearing the body design. The association of the dancer's own body features with those lands, and with the body parts of the original Ancestral Beings which made those lands, is an important aspect of symbolism developed in the ceremony. The Mardayin ceremony has initiatory, mortuary and fertility elements and elaborates the theme of an individual's spiritual association with the ritual property of their clan. Such property includes the clan lands and sacred objects which are thought to be the transformed body parts of the Ancestral Beings. We have seen that paintings of transforming figures can also be used to highlight the transforming properties of the body parts of Ancestral Beings. *Rarrk* x-ray in-fill provides another means of developing this belief. The connection between these two different styles of painting helps to build the logical coherence of the artistic system as a whole.

Western Arnhem Land artists continually create variations on these basic styles of in-fill. For example, they can mix naturalistic x-ray motifs with geometric *rarrk* patterns or with skeletal features. Artists may choose to paint whole figures inside other figures, for example sacred objects inside creator figures or children inside their mothers. These variations on the techniques allow artists to create the more complex symbolic properties of an otherwise stark figurative image.

Conclusion

Western Arnhem Land painting is unique in the way that x-ray in-fill or the representation of the transforming qualities of the Ancestral Beings, help to develop the symbolic aspects of figurative paintings. In eastern Arnhem Land, the most powerful bark paintings are wholly geometric in form, but western Arnhem Land artists create powerful images of the Ancestral Beings using variations of figurative techniques. Western Arnhem Land paintings communicate some of the central ideas in Aboriginal belief and help to maintain knowledge of the Ancestrally created world through the generations. However, the artistic system also provides for the creation of new ways of representing the Ancestral Beings. Such innovation is not inimical to religious beliefs, rather it enlivens Aboriginal religion and helps to incorporate new knowledge about the Ancestral Beings with what is already known.

LUKE TAYLOR

Art and religion in eastern Arnhem Land

PLATE 12
Mutitjpuy
Yirrkala/NT
Fire dreaming 1971
Ochre on bark
160 x 79cm irreg
Djapu Clan
Dhuwa Moiety

In the Dreamtime a Crocodile Man, Baru, succeeded in making a fire for the first time during a Nara ceremony at Blue Mud Bay. One day Baru's wife refused to give him any of the shellfish she was cooking, so he pushed her into the fire where her arms and legs were badly burnt. She changed into a blue-tongued lizard and ran away. In retaliation her clansmen threw hot coals on Baru's back, causing him to jump into the water where he changed into a crocodile. The scars on his back are visible today as the scales of the crocodile.

Here, Baru is depicted in the top panel before he was burnt. In the centre panel, Baru is shown with one of his offspring, with the scale pattern on his back. The diamond pattern in the painting is a clan design associated with Baru, which symbolises fire, as well as his scales. The fish are species that live in the same habitat as Baru.

The paintings and sculptures from eastern Arnhem Land that grace the walls and cases of art galleries throughout the world have their origins in the religious life of the Yolngu people who made them. As far as the Yolngu are concerned, these art works originated through the creative acts of the Ancestral Beings who determined the form of the universe. In order to understand Yolngu art, therefore, it is necessary to place it in its religious context, to show how it is linked to the *Wangarr* (the Ancestral past) and how it is used in ritual. Yet this does not mean that the concept of art has no place in discussions about Yolngu paintings or that there is something fundamentally wrong in referring to them as art. In fact, aesthetic motivations are a part of the reason for many ritual acts, and qualitative judgements are also made about ritual performances and paintings. However it is always important to bear in mind that artists are working within a religious tradition and that art is only part of what they are creating.

Yolngu paintings are manifestations of the Ancestral past, of the Dreaming. The paintings were first made by the Ancestral Beings and then handed on to the human groups who succeeded them in the land. The designs often originated through some Ancestral event. The background design used in some Manggalili paintings from Djarrakpi at Cape Shield provides an example of this. The design consists of a set of parallel wavy lines and represents the marks left on the sand by the receding tide and, in particular, the design it left on the body of an Ancestral Being who was drowned and washed up on the beach. Another example is the diamond design of the Madarpa clan which represents the pattern that was burnt into the back of Bara, the Crocodile, when the bark sheets of his hut went up in flames (Plate 12). In such ways, the designs themselves can be thought of as part of the essence of the Ancestral Beings and, in reproducing these sacred designs in ritual, people are recreating something that belongs to the Dreaming.

Geometric designs lie at the heart of eastern Arnhem Land paintings. Each design is associated with a particular place and the Ancestral events that occurred there. Other elements of the painting elaborate on the mythological geography of the landscape, showing how the form of the world was shaped by the events of the Dreaming. The geometric designs are usually sufficient in themselves to identify a painting, to show that it belongs to a particular clan and that it represents a certain area of land. Paintings which are the property of the group that inherited them from the Ancestral past provide a charter, and almost a condition, for their ownership of the land. For this reason paintings are of political as well as religious significance.

Art has two complementary general roles in Yolngu religion: it is a means of transmitting religious knowledge from generation to generation and it is a means of transferring spiritual power from one generation to the next. The first role is relatively easy to grasp. The paintings represent mythological events and, in learning about paintings, people learn about the Ancestral past. The second role is harder to understand. Paintings are a link with the Ancestral past but they are also a link with the previous generations who used the paintings. Paintings are part of a process that involves the continual conservation and recycling of Ancestral power, and they are also a means of establishing direct contact between an individual and the Ancestral past. The nature of a particular painting depends on the identity of the individual and the purpose of the ceremony. At circumcision, a painting may be done on a boy's chest in order to help build a spiritually powerful person whereas, on death, a painting may be made to help the person's soul return to the sacred waters of his clan's well to rejoin the spiritual dimension.

A boy is painted on several occasions during the years and months leading up to his circumcision (Plate 13). The first time he is painted his body may simply be covered with red ochre. On the next occasion his face may be painted with an elaborate design and his body with red ochre. On the final occasion his body will be covered with red ochre, with an elaborate clan design painted on his chest. Yolngu explain this order of doing things as a conditioning process, as both getting him used to the idea of being painted and also introducing him slowly to the powerful expressions of the Ancestral past. The painting is an important part of the process of establishing the boy's identity as a member of a clan that he is linked to by descent. Often it will be a painting from a place in his own clan's country, but sometimes it will be a place belonging to another closely related clan. The painting also draws attention to him as someone special, a sign that he has left childhood behind and taken a major step towards joining the world of the initiated adult men. Later he will see the sacred objects of his clan and of related clans. These objects are thought to be even more powerful manifestations of the Ancestral Beings than the paintings. As a result of such experiences throughout his life and as he gains in age and wisdom, he also accumulates spiritual power.

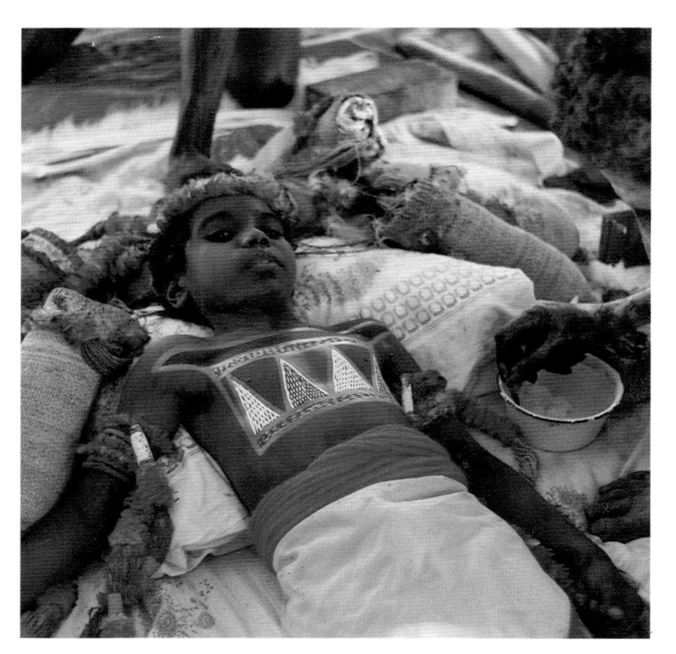

PLATE 13
Young initiate being decorated at Yirrkala.

On a person's death it is important that the soul should return to the clan's Ancestral lands, both for its own sake and to ensure that the spiritual resources of the clan are not diminished. A person's spiritual power is a resource to be handed on eventually to new generations of clan members. Yolngu mortuary rituals are grand affairs almost operatic in their scale. They are structured by a guiding theme, the journey of the dead person's soul from the place of death to its final resting place. It is a journey that is acted out in ritual by performing Ancestral law, by producing dances, songs and paintings that are associated with places along the way. Each event in the funeral is associated with a stage on the journey. The ceremony may, for example, open with a dance that represents Ancestral Beings taking the coffin to the body of the dead person. This acts as an allegory for the Ancestral Beings finding and taking the soul of the man. In the past the dead body was itself painted with designs representing a place on the spirit's journey. Today it is usually the coffin lid that is painted. In painting the coffin lid, people are summoning up the powers of the Ancestral Beings associated with the place represented by the design, so that they will come and take the soul on the next leg of the journey. Painting in this case is clearly a ritual act rather than, for example, a process designed to produce an object of contemplation, for as soon as it is completed the coffin is covered in a cloth and made ready for burial.

The mythological subject of a coffin painting may, however, be taken up in other parts of the ritual and certain meanings elaborated. Another major theme of Yolngu mortuary rituals is the struggle that the soul has in reaching its destination and the hazards of the journey. The coffin painting may represent an allegory of this. For example a coffin painting may include representations of fish in wet season flood waters and fish-eating birds. The fish represents the soul, the water that it struggles through represents the journey; and the bird, the hazards that it is likely to encounter on the way. The theme may be acted out by dancers carrying the coffin on its journey to the grave. In such ways paintings combine with other elements in the creation of metaphors that are appropriate to the objectives of the ritual.

Episodes of the myths of a particular place often are more closely associated with some rituals than with others, as in turn are the paintings that belong to those places. The mythology of Djarrakpi at Cape Shield is closely associated with mortuary rituals. The Guwak (Nightbird), who founded Djarrakpi for the Manggalili clan, confronted his own death in the Dreaming. He saw death ahead and accepted it. Going out to sea in a canoe, he was washed overboard and drowned. In other stories he helped establish a way to the land of the dead for the souls of the Yirritja moiety. Songs and dances of the Guwak are often used to announce a death or begin a mortuary ritual. Nyapililngu, 'sister' to the Guwak, lived in the coastal dunes at Djarrakpi. She used a digging stick to help her walk up and down the sandhills and to dig for tubers in the ground. In paintings and carvings she is sometimes represented just by her digging stick. Nyapililngu mourned her dead brother and placed his drowned body in a sand sculpture called *Yingapungapu.* She sat beside the sand sculpture and in her anguish cut her head with the sharpened end of her digging stick. The sand sculpture is elliptical in form and is used today to contain the pollution associated with a dead body. People preparing a body for burial eat and then bury their food remains within the *Yingapungapu,* thus ensuring that others do not come in contact with it. The sand sculpture is frequently represented in paintings from Djarrakpi and, as well as referring to the mythology of Nyapililngu and the Guwak, it also connotes the uses of the *Yingapungapu* in ritual.

Although art objects are not produced in Yolngu ritual simply to be looked at, their form and visual impact are none the less important factors. There is no easy dichotomy between the aesthetic and ritual function of a painting. Designs in the form of sand sculpture and ceremonial ground often provide the spatial framework for Yolngu ritual. The making of a sand sculpture is a central event of many ceremonies and, once made, it becomes the focal point of ritual action. Painting in some cases sets the pace of Yolngu ritual. The painting process is a slow one. Although in the case of a large object, such as a memorial post, the initial setting of the design may be done quite quickly, it may take several days to complete the painting by covering the surface with a layer of fine cross-hatched lines. An elaborate body painting will not take as long as this, but it will often take most of the day to complete. The painting process must as a consequence provide part of the impact of ritual. At his circumcision ceremony a boy must remain still for several hours at a time while a pattern of fine lines is drawn slowly and methodically across his chest. The place where a painting is being done often marks a place of peace and tranquillity set apart from the more frenzied activities of singing and dancing. And there is no doubt that the intention is to produce something of beauty – something of beauty that is charged with Ancestral power. The technique of cross-hatching results in a painting whose surface shimmers with light and which appears full of movement and life. This brilliance represents the Ancestral power of the painting shining from within.

The changes in Yolngu society brought about by European colonisation have not in any way diminished the role of painting in ceremony, though it has resulted in the disappearance of some types of painting and the development of others. For example today, at death, paintings are rarely made on the dead person's body, but on the coffin lid instead. Another major change has been the production of art for an outside audience, for sale through craft stores and art galleries. However even this is not a wholly secular activity. Bark paintings produced for sale are produced under the same constraints of ownership as other paintings. Moreover, bark painting has provided a major new context for learning about a clan's paintings, and for ensuring that knowledge about the Ancestral past is maintained. However, it also has the effect of widening the audience for the paintings and of persuading the European colonisers of Australia of the religious basis of Arnhem Land society, in order to play a part in its continuing survival.

HOWARD MORPHY

Women's acrylic paintings from Yuendumu

PLATE 14
Bessie Nakamarra
Yuendumu/NT
Wapirti, sweet potato dreaming 1986
Synthetic polymer paint on canvas
99.5 x 53cm
Warlpiri Language Group

This depicts the Wapirti Yam, or Sweet Potato site, from the Mt Singleton area. The women of the Nakamarra and Napurrula subsections dig for the sweet potato.

Three hundred kilometres north-west of Alice Springs, in the desert community of Yuendumu, Warlpiri Aborigines reproduce their ritual life and daily activities in large and vibrant paintings. Like much of the art that comes out of the Central Australian Desert, these canvasses display a core of traditional graphic symbols, including: circles, semi-circles and lines, meanders and dots; animal and human footprints spread across the new-found surface, mimicking the traditional sand-stories which are drawn on the ground during story-telling; paintings on ritual artefacts and body paintings.

But whereas the traditional sand-stories blow away and the body paintings are rubbed off, the canvasses endure. That is because they differ radically in one obvious, in fact, glaring respect. They are of acrylic paint (synthetic polymer paint) – a paint that is seemingly at odds with such traditional pigments as ochre and charcoal. Are they though? Studying these acrylic paints provides a map into the ritual designs that tie the Warlpiri people to their ancestors, to their land and to themselves.

Though several articles and books have been devoted to men's acrylic paintings, there is little mention of women's art. This is not surprising. The anthropological literature on women's ritual – and by implication women's art – is of recent origin. In the last decade the paintings were dominated by men. The reasons are complex, and involve the false assumption by some art advisers and anthropologists that only men contributed to the visual ritual life of the community. This was an extension of anthropological assumptions about the absence of ritual art among women. Only men could reproduce the Dreamings, the logic went, so only men should get the paints and canvas boards.

Historical background

While the Dreamtime stretches into the undatable past, its acrylic representations have a briefer and slightly more exact legacy. It was in the seventies, during the Land Rights Movement, that art advisers and other non-Aborigines supplied the Yuendumu community

PLATE 15
Maggy Napangardi Watson painting her initiated Women's Dreaming, Yuendumu.

with water paints and cardboard, and encouraged the elders, particularly the men, to reproduce in a more permanent medium, the Dreamings they recounted in the sand, on their shields and ritual poles. The paints chosen by the non-Aboriginals represented an attempt to evoke the natural pigments traditionally applied.

Similar experiments were conducted in the nearby settlement of Papunya, where the walls of the school were painted with traditional designs. While Yuendumu's so-called art movement halted, the Papunya painters flourished. It was only after the Warlpiri people at Yuendumu were given acrylic paints, some ten years later, that a sustained effort began.

Initially, the Warlpiri people produced the canvasses and cardboards because they provided a quick and much-needed source of income. The women were allowed to apply acrylic designs to objects of daily use (such as baby carriers and digging sticks). These objects were subsequently sold to non-Aboriginal people working at Yuendumu and to tourists in Alice Springs. Then the women painted ritual objects such as nullah-nullah (fighting sticks), dancing boards and water carriers.

In 1984, thirty of the most senior women of Yuendumu decided to pool their ritual knowledge and produce enough painted objects to purchase a Toyota four-wheel drive. In yet another curious link between traditional and modern, the Toyota was needed to facilitate travelling to sacred sites and to pursue old-style hunting. The women finally turned their talents to canvas. Their small scale entrepreneurship was so successful that acrylic painting soon became a source of revenue for Yuendumu and its outstations.

They first sold their paintings to a few friends and tourists. Yet what started out as a fund-raising venture quickly attracted the attention of art professionals. Moving from trinket-making to flat surfaces, the Aboriginal women gained a wider and, at times, more discriminating audience. In 1985, Darwin and Sydney hosted large exhibitions that featured the women's paintings. And while the Toyota, which was purchased eight months after the project began, soon broke down, the paintings travelled the world.

The ritual power of painting

The acrylic painting has touched more than the pocket-books of the Warlpiri people. In subtle ways it has redefined, and even strengthened the ritual life of Yuendumu. Acrylic painting has redefined who will have the knowledge of the ritual designs and who may paint them. For acrylic painting isn't the solitary action of an isolated artist but rather a collaborating gesture predicated on ritual rights and obligations among the artists who are both close and distant kin. The paintings may bear a single signature to appease European notions of artistic creation, but they are rarely the work of one hand. Bound by the ties of kinship, the women act out their relationships in painting as they do in their ritual and daily lives.

The first women, the elders who initiated acrylic painting among Warlpiri women, shared one thing: ritual power. They were all over 35 years old, and thus had earned the right to participate actively in traditional ceremonies. The painting is initiated by a woman who is given a canvas by the art adviser; she then chooses a Dreaming over which she has rights. Usually, she will engage other relatives to collaborate.

The woman who initiated the painting oversees the production. Indeed, once the symbols are painted the in-filling is often taken over by women with junior ritual status. The procedure is generally controlled by the elder women so that the production parallels traditional creation. The process of production replicates the traditional way of painting any surface. Whether artists use brushes instead of fingers, or wooden sticks, doesn't change the general procedure.

These elder women ensure that the designs are properly executed, and that laws of secrecy are not violated. During the painting, the elders often recount the stories that the symbols depict. Thus, the painting process has become a conduit for the informal transmission of ritual information. Yet even these stories might reveal just one level of the painting's meaning. For among the Warlpiri people knowledge is power, and it is a power earned only with time and experience in the ritual performances.

Women sometimes even erase paintings when their peers make it clear to them that they are 'giving away' too much knowledge. In particularly sensitive stories, modifications are made by the elder women. A circle might become a semi-circle, a U-shape might be replaced by a line. But such modifications are rare; secret Ancestral designs do not vary markedly from public pictorial arrangements, and the subtle changes may not take place. But the art adviser, who collects the story, will be told very little, so the sacred-secret is not revealed.

The major difference is determined by who is reading the narrative. Only the initiated can decode the more profound Dreamings locked in the canvas and often only the painter herself will know.

What do they mean?

Extensive study, beginning in the 1950s with the work of Nancy Munn, has been directed at the traditional symbols found in Warlpiri art. These symbols have changed little with the medium of acrylic paint, nor have the meanings. What has changed (as has the society as a whole) however, is the nature of the stories that emerge from these symbols and the recent inclusion of more representational icons.

In the most general terms, the shapes found in acrylic paintings, like their predecessors, often represent that mysterious and often intangible world of Dreamings. They are not abstract symbols randomly dispatched across the canvas. To the knowledgeable elders, the dots and dashes offer as much narrative possibility as Morse code. And yet they provide more. The women's acrylic paintings can be read as maps of ritual Dreaming sites, as musical scores for ritual songs, and they can be viewed as representations which, when fully understood, evoke places, animals, dreams, smells and stories that bond the Warlpiri people to their ancestors, to their land and to each other (Plate 16).

Take the circle, the most common element of Warlpiri iconography. It is no mere line continued till it ends where it began, having all its parts equidistant from a common centre. It is, instead, a waterhole or a tree, a ceremonial site, a cave or a combination of those things read at different levels. And a line is more than a longitudinal extension; it can be a person, a tree, a path, an animal, a digging stick.

The symbols are the building blocks of Warlpiri myth. Placed in knowledgeable hands, they can evoke the mythic tale of the Honey Ant, which is the main Dreaming for the site of Yuendumu. In the hands of the uninitiated, they are just dots and dashes.

Why acrylic?

And yet the question still remains, why did the women of Yuendumu reject the watercolours that could more accurately (to the western eye) duplicate the traditional paintings? One of the reasons may be purely practical. Water-based paint requires a regulated mixture of ingredients and is difficult to apply in a dusty desert community. But that doesn't explain the choice of the luminescent colours that characterise Yuendumu art. On a technical level, the shiny paint is similar to the oil and animal fat that is rubbed on the body before it is painted and similar to the shiny look of the best ochres mined in the Central Desert. Perhaps a more subtle answer can be found in the Warlpiri people's response to surface shininess in general. This is considered a sign of health, well-being and beauty, and recalls the Ancestral Beings completely beautified when they originally emerged from the Ancestral ground.

Though the colours are artificial and shiny, this doesn't deny their links to the traditional pigments. The dark background that characterises all acrylic painting is a natural adaptation of the monochrome backgrounds of traditional designs (red and black). The dark skin on which body paintings are placed, or the dark red earth used in sand-stories and sand paintings, find parallels in the dark base colour of acrylic paintings. The jet black acrylic paint, for example, parallels the traditional charcoal and is often more shiny. The white acrylic paint is a more vibrant version of pipe clay. The bright reds and yellows are acrylic equivalents of the natural ochres mined in the Central Australian Desert. The dots were not traditionally used by women but by men. Some ten years ago, the men 'gave' to women the rights to use dots in their acrylic paintings. When the acrylic painting movement first flourished at Yuendumu the main differences between men's paintings and women's paintings were the representations of their respective Ancestral designs. But more specifically, to the uninitiated public, the dots were different. Men's paintings had bigger dots, as big as when they applied dots with natural pigments on their ritual objects and in their body paintings. Women, however, took great care to fill in the space with smaller dots and display a wider range of colours. Also, at the beginning, some women who had lived at Papunya influenced the first steps of their Yuendumu relatives to use smaller dots. The colours of the dots depend on the taste of the artists, but generally the painting as a whole must be vibrant and radiant. The artists search for these qualities when 'filling' the space with dots, choosing the colours for the dots carefully.

The very foreignness of acrylic paint has allowed the women of Yuendumu to experiment in ways that were impossible before.

This versatility allows the women to merge different Dreamings and different media. For example, some of the acrylic paints depict parts of stories of certain sites, mixtures of sand-stories, paintings on ritual artefacts and body paintings. This complicates the anthropologist's task of decoding the paintings. But if in one way acrylic paint has made the job of the anthropologist more difficult, it has also helped. For stories painted in acrylic, unlike a painting on a ceremonial dancing board, provide a permanent record of what for thousands of years has been rubbed off after each ceremonial performance.

The acrylic painting movement has further expanded the repertoire of stories now told. Acrylic paintings are not simply limited to the Dreamtime. Recent canvasses have added new subjects – the arrival of a satellite dish, and the passage of Halley's Comet to the traditional Dreamings.

The observations of anthropologist Levi-Strauss on the changes both in traditional and western art find particular application to the situation among Yuendumu painters. Cognizant of the crises that confront 'tribal' communities, he predicted that such transformation 'might well consist in the birth of another type of art.' (1973:281)

The acrylic painting movement testifies both to a crisis and a new type of art, which is neither purely traditional nor modern. The crisis, of course, was economic. The original inspiration for the women's paintings was the purchase of a four-wheel drive vehicle. But that financial motivation in no way detracts from the power of the acrylic paintings themselves.

Though it is unknown to the uninitiated observer, the paintings that hang in non-Aboriginal galleries are born out of a debate that took place back in Yuendumu when the painting movement began. What could be painted into the canvasses, and what had to be left out, was often vigorously discussed so that secret ritual knowledge would not be transmitted.

This is not 'tribal' art. This is an art which testifies to the Aboriginal mythological heritage and to the current state of the Aboriginal community. The collaboration may not be apparent, nor the debate and ritual legacy contained on the canvas, but the power and aesthetic virtue remains even for the uninitiated. It does not require ritual knowledge at all to lose oneself in the infinity of the acrylic dots.

FRANÇOISE DUSSART

PLATE 16
Mavis Napangati
Papunya/NT
Bush onion story 1987
Synthetic polymer paint
on canvas
151 x 120cm
Luritja Language Group

A Yarlka or Bush Onion story from Karrinyarra (central Mt Wedge), west of Alice Springs, is depicted here. The women ('U' shapes) are shown digging up the bush onions and putting them into coolamons (oval shapes). The short bars are the women's digging sticks, while the circles depict the Yarlka Dreaming site at Mt Wedge. The background colours symbolise the Yarlka flowers after the rain.

PLATE 16

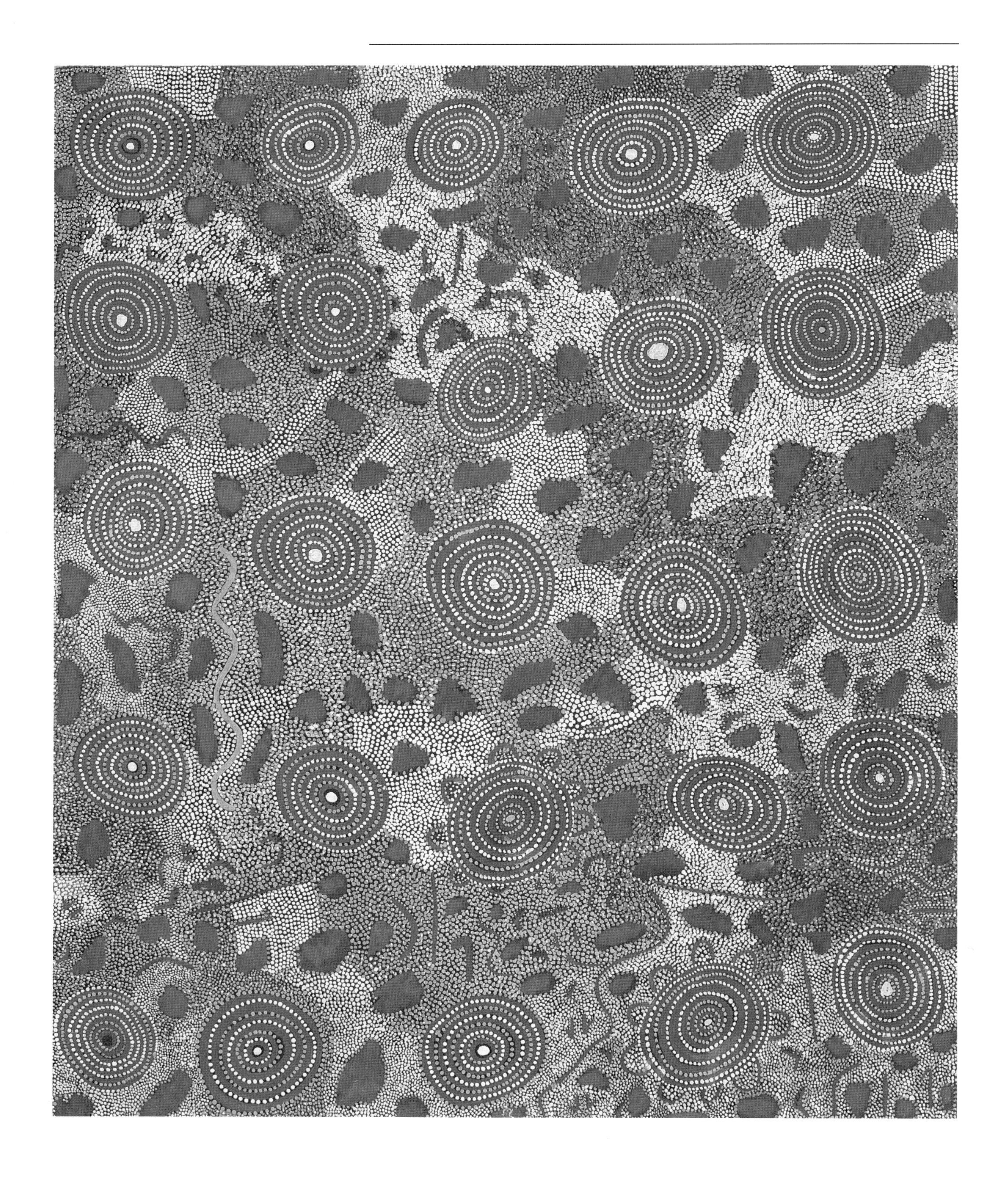

'Make 'im flash, poor bugger'

Talking about men's painting in Papunya

PLATE 17
Johnny Wararrngula Tjupurrula
Papunya/NT
Tjingarri events 1981
Synthetic polymer paint on canvas
185.5 x 153.4cm
Luritja Language Group

Events which occurred during the Dreamtime at the site of Tjikarri, a ceremonial cave north-west of the Ehrenburg Range, are referred to in this painting. At this site (represented by the circle) a group of Ancestral Tjingarri Men performed a ceremony. Before starting, they lit a fire so they could flush out enough game to have a feast during the ritual. The brown patches in the painting indicate the burnt bushland.

In the meantime, the aggressive Nyananyana 'devil' people were camping nearby and attacked a group of Mala Hare Wallaby people who had journeyed to the site from the west. The Nyananyana chased the Mala people underground and when peace was restored, the ceremony of the Tjingarri commenced. The tracks of the Mala are depicted, along with their weapons such as spears, axes and boomerangs. The ceremonial items of the Tjingarri Men, like hair-string belts, are also depicted.

We have been driving through the bush all day, the last four or five hours in an interminably slow four-wheel drive across spinifex and soft sand, then into the dune country. We are 'close up' now, and the old man is growing restless. Johnny Wararrngula Tjupurrula, an accomplished and distinctive member of the Papunya Tula artists group, is coming back to look at his country, to one of the most important sites of all, Tjikarri in remote central Australia, 480 kilometres west of Alice Springs. Tjikarri has provided the inspiration for some of Wararrngula's most spectacular paintings – complex overlays of dots and patterns that dance in front of you, that give you a feeling of being able to look deep into the canvas, set against multiple foreground symbols of water, food and fire, the overall work conveying a sense of rich life-sustaining power. The wheels spin over the ridge of the last dune and we are there. But it is not much – a rocky outcrop much like any other, perhaps even more ordinary than many that we have passed during the long day. The rockholes turn out to be dry and there's effectively nothing in the way of edible plant food; all the animal tracks are old so there will be no fresh meat tonight. And yet the old man is taken away by it; he is crying, he is talking, singing to the rock, he is calling out its names, its stories and he's clambering, almost crawling, over the rock face, this way and that way, stroking, rubbing, feeling his country. For the next twenty-four hours, late into the night and all the next day back to Papunya, it is as if he is in another world, ceaselessly telling the stories of the events and the creatures that passed through here and forged this landscape. But more than just telling them he seems to be living them, and actually seeing them still visible in the forms in front of him.

'Nyawa rakula ngaatja Nga̲nkurru kapi yun̲ngu ngarrinyi. Ngaan̲i Mala tjut̲a yanu. Ngaakutu Tjikarrikutu wati ngalyanu tjukurrpa Mala tjut̲a Palkuwanatjanu. Kala, tjana nyinangi Nyananyana tjut̲a Tjikarringka, kutu nyinapayiya ngaangka. Tjana Nyananyana tjut̲a Tjikarringka pika patan̲angi tjanampa. Paluru ilalpiya nyinangu Kala wati Mala tjut̲a ngalyanu nyarra talingka Tjikarrikutu. Yuwa, palunyatjanu paluru pikarringu, Nyananyana tjut̲a wati Mala tjut̲a uwankarra pikarringu. Kala pikarringkula wiyarringkula tjananyalpi tjarrpatjunu. Tjana tjarrpangu Nyananyanawati tjut̲a, tjananya pil̲untanu, pil̲untanu kutu. Paluru tjana ngula ngula pakan̲u, Mala tjut̲a pakan̲u Mawurrungula. Palulanguruya yanu wan̲malingku Ulurulakutu. Tjukurrpa ngaatja punyunyuku, watjalpayilatjut jananya.'

'See this rockhole, it's called "Ngan̲kurru," there's water inside. The Mala (Hare Wallaby) people went through here. These Dreamtime Mala people came to Tjikarri from the Balgo area. But the Nyananyana people always camp at Tjikarri and they were waiting here to fight the Mala mob. The Mala people came up close, they approached Tjikarri through that sand country. Yes, and they all fought together, the Nyananyana devils and the Mala people. And when they finished fighting, the Nyananyana mob made the Mala go under the ground. They were stamping that Mala mob right into the ground. The Mala people came up out of the ground a little bit later, over at Mawurrungu. From there they went all the way down to Ayers Rock. This is a story that we teach the young men.' (Plate 17).
Johnny Wararrngula Tjupurrul̲a. *Mala Tjukurrpa* (1987).

Talk to the Papunya Tula artists about what motivates their contemporary painting and they will answer as if with one voice: they paint for their 'Dreamings,' those sacred stories of their country that account for its forms, its inhabitants and its produce (Plate 18). In Western Desert language, the first language of most of the Papunya painters, the term for such stories is *tjukurrpa.* And when you talk to a painter about a particular work he will first of all tell you (as far as the constraints of religious secrecy allow) about the *tjukurrpa,* which is the painting's source. He will tell you the specific interpretation which the symbols assume in this story. He will point you to the tract of country in which the story takes place, often naming the sites in great detail, and he will talk about the custodianship of the area where the story is centered, naming both specific contemporary custodians and the particular subsections of the kin system through whom ownership is generally passed down. For the artists, this is the essential background information to the proper understanding and appreciation of their work. Most of this information is, of course, not translated onto the canvas itself and paintings only rarely attempt to function as coherent narratives of the underlying *tjukurrpa,* normally representing instead, only a few key elements. But the point is that the purpose and validity of a painting lies in its Dreaming. To the Papunya artists, and the society in which they live and work, a painting not informed by a Dreaming (if such a thing were seriously possible) would be nothing more than frivolous decoration; simply not art.

These *tjukurrpa* provide interpretations of the land that verify and reaffirm traditional Aboriginal law. It is through these stories that the law is visible and accessible. Thus when a Papunya Tula artist paints a contemporary work he sees himself as part of the unbroken cultural tradition of the artist; as an instrument through which the old established law is retransmitted and renewed, whether it be in sand painting, body painting, canvas or whatever. Dinny Nolan Tjampitjinpa, in discussing a Water Dreaming which he's painted on a Papunya door, explains it like this:

'Yalatji yara ngaa tjut̲a luuwa kampatjatjarra. Nyuntu riitarrinytjaku piintingi ngaatjut̲a. Yan̲angu irrit̲itja tjut̲angku yara nintin̲u.

Kapi yutuwari Kal̲ipinpalanguru Watupinypalawana kul̲pangu. Parra yanu Yarrupunulanguru tjarrpangu Mikanytjila. Yun̲tumula maa ngarringi yalinytjarrawana. Kapi paluru maa kul̲pangu kutukutju, tjarrpangulpi Mikanytjila, wilurarra tjarrpangu.'

'This is how it is – these stories are the law that controls the canvas. You have to read these paintings. These are the stories that the old people knew.

The rain cloud came back from Kal̲ipinpa and went past Watupinypa. It went around from Yarrupunu and into Mikanytji. It lay along the north over Yuendumu. Then it returned finally to Mikanytji, forever, going in on the west side.'
Dinny Nolan Tjampitjinpa. *Tjakulpa Kuwarritja* (1987).

It is difficult for white people to appreciate the interconnections between religious belief, ceremonial knowledge and the relationship with the land that contribute to the Aboriginal perception of the function of contemporary painting. And many of us, looking to the havoc that contact with Western society has brought to much of Aboriginal culture, are concerned that the West's current infatuation with central Australian art might bring with it similar disastrous consequences. This is not a concern which at the moment is shared by the Papunya artists. On the contrary, unworried by the artistic innovations which the medium of canvas has given rise to, and with the

PLATE 18
Pintubi Men's painting camp, Papunya

problem of possible revelation of secret-sacred material sorted out many years ago, the artists see their rise to Western popularity as perfectly in accord with Aboriginal tradition.

Acclaim by white society is simply endorsement by a foreign, albeit economically dominant culture, of an activity that, for the Aboriginal people, has its own legitimacy. And in a community which exists mostly on welfare cheques, large payments for paintings have failed to create significant economic divisions. Profits from paintings become dispersed among relatives according to the culture's established network of obligations or are put into shared and normally short-lived resources such as cars, television sets and videos. Prizes and other honours conferred by white society are no doubt a matter of individual pride and pleasure, but have no impact on that individual's status as determined by internal Aboriginal politics and ceremony.

In particular it is worthwhile trying to understand, especially in a year in which Australians are being asked to celebrate the 200th anniversary of the invasion of the continent, the role of modern painting in affirming Aboriginal ownership of their country. The actual strategies through which land ownership is assigned are too complicated to discuss here, but we can say broadly that each central Australian has hereditary rights over and above obligations towards certain tracts of land. While non-painting relatives may sometimes authorise him to represent their sites, and on other occasions he may co-operate with other artists in a joint work that has wider scope, an artist will normally only paint Dreamings associated with sites from within his rightful country. For although Dreaming tracks, that is the paths followed by the mytholical Ancestral Beings, cover vast areas, each *tjukurrpa* has a highly localised focus, which centres upon and is regarded as being essentially about, one specific site. Each site, of course, may have a number of different *tjukurrpa* focussed upon it. Painting the Dreamings of a site, then constitutes tangible evidence that one is sufficiently well educated in the Aboriginal view of the world to be able to take up one's inherited rights. Painting is proof that the artist knows the Dreamings, which in turn is proof that he knows the law, and this establishes that he is worthy to be a guardian of his country. Rather than operating as 'mnemonics' for their source *tjukurrpa* (canvasses are far too sparing and selective in their depiction of elements from the story to have any real function as keys to memory), they are seen to operate as demonstrations of the power and propriety of one's knowledge. Contemporary acrylic paintings thus join the older more traditional methods such as dance performance, song cycles and body decoration, by which Aboriginal people show each other that they know their business.

Of equal importance these days is the artists' perception of 'whitefella' responses to these proofs of land ownership that constitute the canvasses. This concept of religious performance as uncontestable evidence of rights to land is so ingrained that for the artists it is almost inconceivable that it could not also be an integral part of white morality. Ironically, perhaps at a time when even the most fundamental aspects of black land rights are hotly contested in our parliaments, when you witness, admire and purchase a canvas, you are seen to be confirming that white society at large recognises the basic proposition underlying the work – that Aboriginal people are the inalienable owners of this country.

This much having been said about the traditional role of the modern art movement, it is worth repeating the point that the Papunya Tula art is decidedly not merely traditional work transposed onto canvas. Of course the contemporary work employs traditional symbols and in many ways imitates traditional textures, but in the fifteen years or so since the founding of the movement the canvasses have taken on a unique look. This markedly new style, a modern selection and extension of ancient elements, can be seen as a response, in both artistic and broader cultural terms, to the nature of canvas itself as a medium of expression. The major innovations which constituted this response took place very quickly following the founding of the movement in 1970-71. Many of the initial efforts on canvas were largely direct representations of ceremonial art or of ceremony itself: body designs, detailed head-dress constructions and depictions of figures engaged in ritual. Some of this early work attempted to duplicate important religious art. This included replication of sacred painted stones, copies of engravings and contours from ceremonial shields and, in a few cases, almost photographic representations of rock art normally restricted to viewing only by the initiated men. Unlike the modern work, these paintings presented their aspects of ceremonial life against plain dark backgrounds (Plate 19).

Perhaps because the artists were so pleased with what they were achieving in the new medium, they were at first oblivious to some of its consequences. Principal among these, was that paintings on canvas were not covered by the long-established rules that guaranteed the secrecy of the rituals and artefacts that they were now depicting. Canvasses were not guarded and restricted from view through the same laws and authority structures that protected sacred stones, for example. Neither were they ritually destroyed at the end of a ceremony in the same way as secret sand mosaics and body designs. On the contrary, canvas had introduced a concept of art as public and permanent.

PLATE 19
Kaapa Tjampitjinpa
Papunya/NT
Kangaroo story 1971
Synthetic polymer paint on composition board
121 x 80.5cm irreg
Anmatyerre Language Group

This painting is characteristic of some of the early Papunya paintings, where representational elements are combined with non-representational symbols. This painting relates to a Kangaroo Dreaming site at Mt Dennison and its associated ceremony. The central circle is the site. The path taken by the Kangaroo Men is represented by the vertical line of tracks. Ceremonial items can be seen in the corners of the picture. (Permission to exhibit this painting was obtained from the artist.)

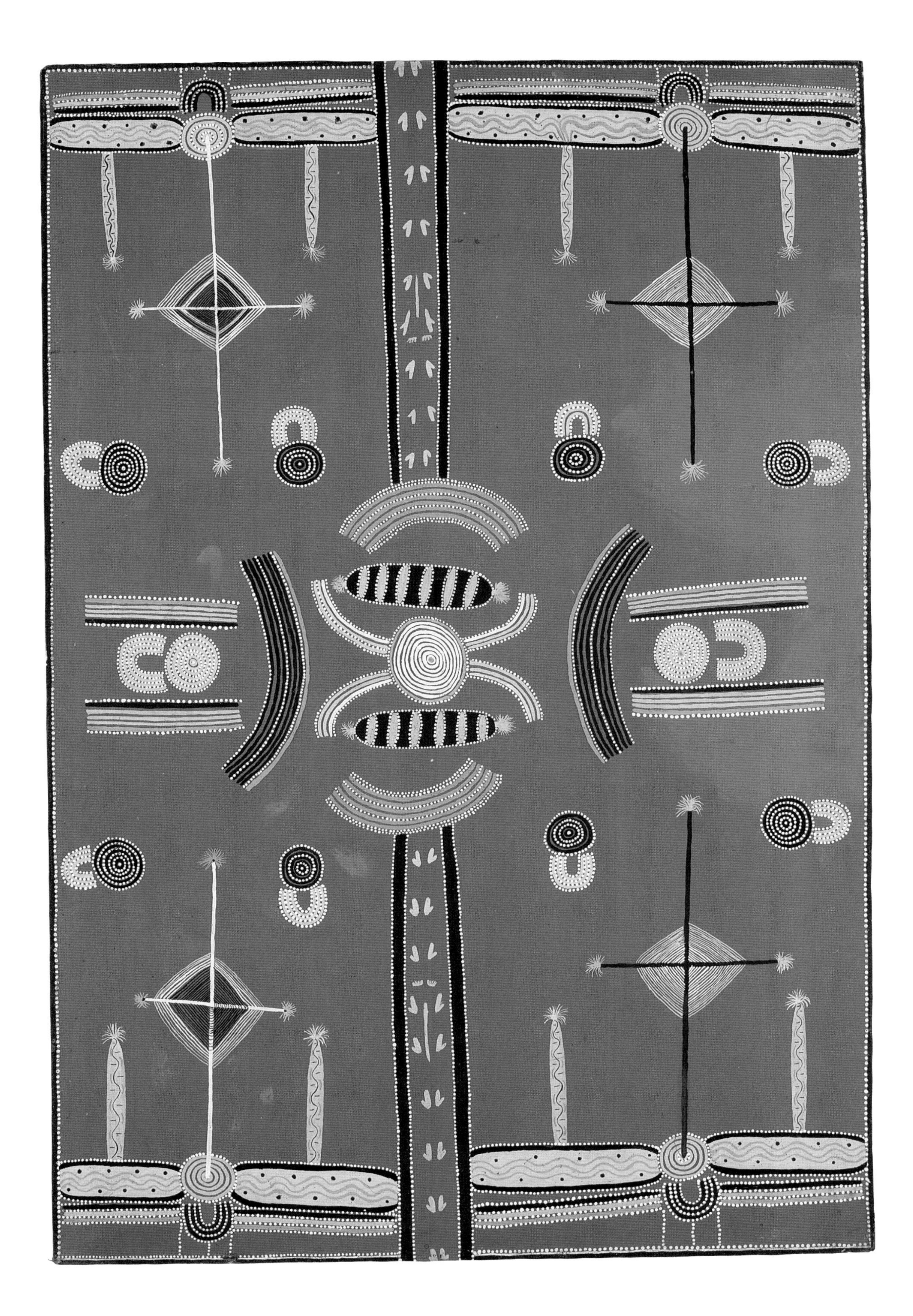

This concept was in direct conflict with the initial practice of the male artists, and there was consternation in the communities when it was realised that secret-sacred material was in danger of being revealed. The appropriate changes were made very quickly. Most naturalistic depictions of humans, animals and their Dreamtime progenitors were eliminated; there were no more depictions of figures actually participating in ritual, or duplications of sacred objects. Design elements which might betray secret patterns were also deleted. Thus developed a consensus on the set of traditional symbols that could be safely used for publicly displayed work – for instance, the concentric circles that have various meanings (such as a camp, soakage, fire or hill); animal tracks; 'U' shapes representing humans sitting in the sand, wind breaks, breasts; and wavy lines symbolising flowing water or rising smoke, snakes and so on. With this set of symbols, capable of being interpreted in a variety of ways, all kinds of stories could be depicted. Even secret stories could be painted without giving the uninitiated a window to the secret ceremonial world of the men.

But this response should not be seen simply as a reduction in the inventory of representations available for painting. The artists faced a considerable challenge. The new medium effectively resulted in an art that could be removed from its functional ceremonial context and become more of an end in itself. Artistic endeavour, regardless of the medium, was still absorbed into the ritual tradition, but it now resulted in a permanent final product, a product whose very nature determined that it should be displayed, sold, viewed and responded to, independent of the ceremonies that traditionally accompanied art work and of the culture and country that gave it meaning. While this necessitated restrictions on the revelation of sacred material it also called for an artistic response. The rectangular (or occasionally circular) frame of the canvas may have liberated artists from some of the constraints imposed by the traditional surfaces – such as human contours or rock shapes – and the new technique made readily accessible a wide range of colours and brushes. But this expansion of possibilities seemed to bring with it one important demand: that if art was to be an end in itself then each painting should be in itself more of a complete vision, not just an aspect of ceremony but a more holistic perception of what ceremony is all about.

The aesthetic response to this was the development of the dotting technique which, although exploited in very different ways by individual painters, is now the hallmark of Papunya Tula canvasses. In place of the initial dark backgrounds the prominent symbols were balanced against patterns of dots These varied in size and in colour and were sometimes overlaid, resulting in some startling optical effects. The dots often comprised not only the background, but the atomic constituents of both the story symbols and the juxtaposed patterns, the symbols sometimes seeming to arise out of the dots as one views the painting. Dotting is of course part of traditional technique and has a role, for example, in body design, where dots tend to be placed in a much more linear and comparatively simplistic fashion than is the case with modern canvasses. The primary inspiration for modern dotting seems rather to have

PLATE 20
Paddy Carrol Jungarrayi painting dots on canvas, Papunya

been the traditional sand mosaics. These tend to be extensive co-operative works, constructed on the ground only for special ceremonies, and made up of pulverised and dyed animal and vegetable matter, placed down piece by piece, or dot by dot as it were. The dots of contemporary canvasses no doubt mimic the atomic technique and the contours of these sand mosaics. However, the increased individual control that painting on canvas brings, and its accessibility to a more distinctive individual extension, interpretation and reworking (in addition perhaps to pragmatic factors such as the ready availability of multi-coloured acrylic paints) have allowed for modern dotting to develop complex interplays of patterns and colours. These effects are neither appropriate, nor easily possible, in the technology of ceremonial sand mosaics.

Of the artists' own conception of this development of their work we know very little. Of the icons, the mythology and anthropology of the paintings we have, with the willing co-operation of the artists, become relatively well informed over the years. But this is to concentrate, in a sense, on the bones at the expense of the flesh of the paintings. It is good that we are at a stage where we can appreciate the essential structure and intelligence of the work. However the appeal of the paintings to our eyes lies as much in the manner in which they have been, so to speak, fleshed out, as in their Dreaming representations: the geometry of the dots, their optical and multi-dimensional effects, striated earth tones that evoke a sense of desert vastness and the interplay of odd patterns and bands of colour.

Some commentators (e.g. Brody 1985, Crocker 1983) suggest that the patterning of the paintings has a topographical or cartographical function, that the patterning is some type of response to the contours of the country and the distribution of sites as perceived from an aerial perspective. This is perhaps possible, but certainly no naturalistic mapping function can be attributed to the paintings. The representation of sites in paintings is rarely to scale; moreover, sites which are represented are often radically misaligned from their natural disposition. In addition, and surprisingly in a culture that requires your knowledge of north and south to be as automatic as breathing, the canvasses have no necessary directional orientation. And there has been no effective demonstration that the geometry of any particular work has any correspondence with natural geometry at all. To questions about such interpretations of their art the artists remain impervious, perhaps uninterested, perhaps just mystified.

The country's contours have surely exercised some influence on the art of these central Australians, but to explain their patternings away as simple attempts to reproduce physical contours is to do a disservice both to the level of abstraction at which they work and to the depth of their vision. The patterning gives life, depth and movement to the story elements of the painting. It provides us with direct visual access to the artists' feelings for those organising forces, in all their richness and multiplicity, which lie beneath the emptiness of the country and, out of which, it has emerged. It is not so much physical as metaphysical.

At the western end of the Mt Liebig Range old Paddy Tjangala, ngangkari (traditional healer), artist and boss-man for this country, sits by the Tjintirrtjintirr (Willie Wagtail) Dreaming site, singing songs and reciting stories over the sacred stone of Amunturrngu:

'Pul̲i ngaatja Tjangala ngalipilinya. Kanyin̲in̲a pul̲i ngaatja, tjamu ngayuku, tjamu ngalimpa. Tjukurrpa watjalkun̲anta Tjangala ngaatjarra. Ngaakutu ngalyanu kuunyi.'

'This stone is called Tjangala, just like you and me. I look after this stone – he's my grandfather, our grandfather. I'll tell you the Dreaming for this Tjangala, how he came here, poor thing.'

And although the stone is like nothing in the landscape – its smoothness, its deep brown half-shine, its weight, the sound it makes when tapped, giving it the atmosphere of something alien or supernatural – Paddy halts for a second. Leaning forward he dips his finger into some red ochre and paints one rough finger-width stroke across the stone. There's a shadow of a smile across his face, maybe from pleasure, maybe from a private joke. He turns and says (in English), 'Oh, make 'im flash, poor bugger.'

Paddy's simple gesture here I think captures the aesthetic impulse behind Papunya art. To European eyes, central Australia can present some incredibly beautiful sights – we do love mountains after all, and there are sunsets over the desert dunes that take our collective breaths away. We are so well socialised into these concepts of beauty that it is hard for us to believe that they do not translate at all into Western Desert culture. For our notions of beauty are not those of the Tula artists, with whom I have travelled the bush, and they are not reflected in their works of art. Their culture does not value, at least in its attitude to the land and its art, that beauty which is merely attraction to external physical form. The beauty of a landscape lies instead in one's belonging to it, in one's unbreakable ties with the Dreamtime Beings who constitute it – sympathy for their sufferings, reverence for their antiquity and celebration of the life-sustaining elements that they provide. Papunya Tula canvasses are visions, not of, but from within the landscape. They are testaments to the richness of a culture that has taken this arid 'poor bugger' of a desert and made it into a representation of abundant overflowing life.

IAN GREEN

The economic basis for cultural reproduction

PLATE 21 (opposite)
Jack Wunuwun
Gamedi Outstation/
Maningrida/NT
Fishtrap story 1984
Ochre on bark
82 x 135cm irreg
Djinang Language Group
Gang-Ngarl Clan

The conical fishtrap, mandjabu *is still used by fishermen in central Arnhem Land to catch fish, mainly barramundi and salmon catfish. It is used by wedging the trap into a trapping fence built across a tidal creek at low tide. When the tide begins to run out the fish are forced into the mouth of the trap and cannot escape. The trap is made with a detachable inner mouth which prevents the fish from swimming out. These are depicted as the small conical shapes in the painting. On another level, the fish trap is related to mortuary beliefs, in which the journey of the soul to its final resting place is likened to the hazardous path of a fish.*

Painting is hard work, half inspiration, half perspiration

The economic and religious components of Aboriginal life are often separated for analytical purposes and referred to as the economic and cultural systems. In reality, however, they are closely connected and interdependent. The belief system influences economic decisions and the economic system influences culture. In Aboriginal society today these systems remain closely interrelated and are strongly influenced by traditional practices. However, such interdependence is frequently over-looked when people view and even buy Aboriginal art. All too often, culture is regarded as somehow independent of economic concerns, yet the maintenance of Aboriginal art today is dependent on its role in the Aboriginal economy of northern Australia. Also the cultural meaning of art cannot be divorced from its economic meaning and significance.

For many Aboriginal people who produce artefacts for sale, art is an important component of their livelihood. For the artistic systems to survive, for traditions to be passed from one generation to the next, for the reproduction of this cultural form, it is important that the commercial viability of the art and craft industry is assured now and in the future.

The commercialisation of art has played, and will continue to play, a significant role in its reproduction. A recent ABC radio series 'Being Aboriginal' began with a program in October 1987 entitled 'Without Artists There Is No Culture.' While this statement may be overstating the case there can be no doubt that a significant proportion of Aboriginal culture that is readily available to the wider Australian community, is incorporated in visual art. Increasingly this art is being recognised as a unique component of the Australian heritage that must be encouraged now, to ensure its future survival for the benefit of all Australians.

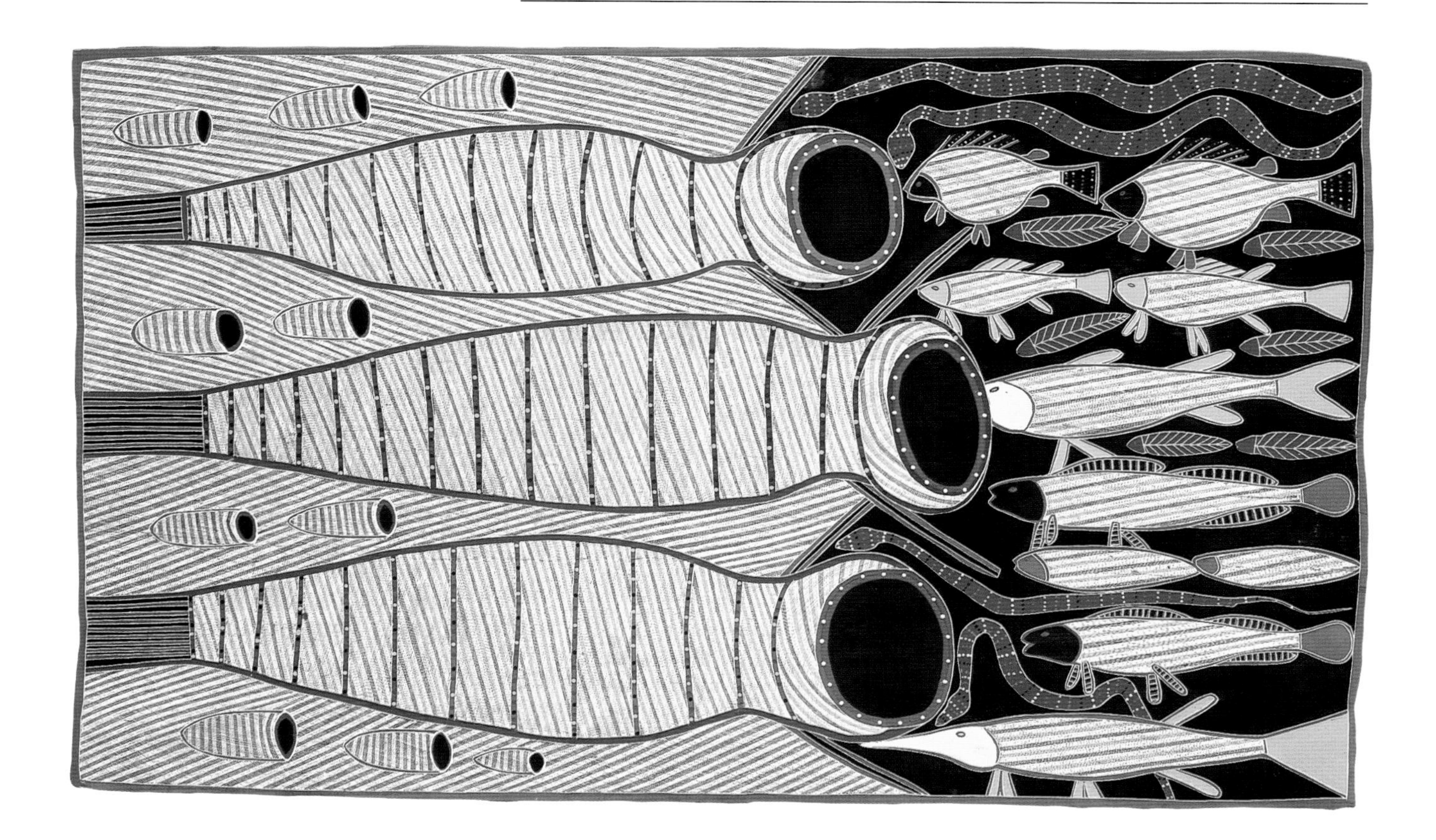

The producers are professionals

While looking at an Aboriginal bark painting or desert canvas, it is easy to forget that its distant producer is a professional artist or artisan who is creating these items for a living. To begin with, it is important to provide some general information on the producers.

The producers: who are they, where are they?

The Aboriginal Arts Board of the Australia Council estimates that 5,000 Aboriginal people in northern and central Australia are involved in artefact manufacture. The majority of these producers (possibly up to 80 per cent) live at small Aboriginal communities called outstations or homelands that are located on Aboriginal land.

It has been suggested that artefact production for sale has increased markedly with the growth in the outstations movement over the past decade and a half. This is partly because the movement has been associated with a strong Aboriginal cultural revival; it is also because the movement has involved a withdrawal from mainstream economic opportunities. At outstations there are no formal employment opportunities and few ways to supplement cash incomes beyond welfare entitlements or the limits set by the job creation schemes.

PLATE 22
Waiting for payment at the Maruku Arts and Crafts shop at Uluru.

PLATE 23
Yolngu women with pandanus weavings made for sale at Batchelor.

The economic significance of artefact production

Despite the attention that the Aboriginal artefact industry has attracted in recent years, there is little information on its economic significance. There is certainly no doubt that a handful of well known artists make a reasonable income from the sale of art, although even the top artists rarely earn more than a few thousand dollars per annum. Recently, the Australian National Gallery procured a bark painting by the Arnhem Land artist, Jack Wunuwun (Plate 21); this is believed to be the first individual piece procured for a five figure sum. In comparison to many white Australian artists, the returns to Aboriginal artists are meagre.

This is apparent in available information on average returns to artists and artisans. In two surveys I conducted at outstations in the Maningrida region I found that art and craft income only accounted for 14 per cent of cash income in 1979 and 6 per cent of cash in 1980. Data from the period 1978-80 indicated that, on average, males earned $288 per annum and females $74. More recent data shows that, on average, producers living on the Pitjantjatjara lands in central Australia earn only $180 per annum from artefact sales. At the Mutitjulu community located in Uluru National Park, in 1985-86, female producers earned an average $666 per annum and males $224. While there is variability in the amount earned by producers (depending on whether they work full-time, part-time or occasionally), only a small number earn more than $2,000 per annum. The most prolific producer at Uluru National Park earned $3,800 over a 58-week period, for 536 intricately carved wooden animals and bowls. The piece rate or hourly rate of return for artefact production is frequently very low.

The economic significance of artefact production far exceeds its proportional contribution to total cash. The two main sources of income at outstations are welfare transfers from the state and returns from subsistence production. The former provides people with cash, while the latter provides what is called an imputed income because it has a market replacement value. While people at many outstations can reduce their dependence on cash and imported goods by engaging in hunting and gathering activities. Artefact manufacture and sale, frequently provides the only means to increase cash incomes above the limits set by social security payments. This manufacturing sector is many outstation people's only source of supplementary cash.

The distribution of production skills

A high proportion of the adult Aboriginal population living at outstations engages in art and craft

PLATE 23

manufacture. In central Arnhem Land, between December 1978 and September 1980, I found that 67 per cent of all adult men and women at outstations produced some artefacts for sale, while 24 per cent produced artefacts for sale in the township. In central Australia, for thirteen months from April 1985, 645 people or 54 per cent of people living on Pitjantjatjara lands sold artefacts to Maruku Arts and Crafts at Uluru. These figures show that an extraordinarily high proportion of the Aboriginal population, particularly at outstations, have the skills to produce artefacts for sale. They also show that there are no barriers preventing Aboriginal people from participating in this industry.

The future supply of producers

Information collected in Arnhem Land demonstrates a direct correlation between the age of producers and their importance in the production of art – not only owing to the ritual knowledge of older people, but also to their ability to present designs in an 'outside' or secular context for widespread viewing. It seems that people only become major producers as they become older and ritually senior, and have less participation in time-consuming hunting and gathering activities.

There is certainly statistical evidence that the numbers of producers increase when market opportunities expand. At the Mutitjulu community for example, there were only 18 producers in 1984-85. This increased to 48 or 60 per cent of the adult population when a new craft outlet was established in 1986. Similar increases occurred in northern Australia when new craft outlets like Mimi Arts and Crafts in Katherine and Waringarri Arts in Kununurra were established. Because the skills for producing artefacts are well distributed, supply will increase rapidly when there is an immediate demand for artefacts. There are also indications that with market demand, innovative designs and art forms will emerge.

Artefact manufacture and the outstation movement

In recent years there has been a shift towards recognising the re-emergence of an 'Aboriginal economy' at outstations. Influential government reports – the Miller Report, 1985, and the Blanchard Homelands report, 1987 – acknowledge that hunter-gatherer activities and artefact manufacture are crucial for the economic viability of outstations.

In these areas where people choose to live on their land and pursue a 'modified traditional' lifestyle, the manufacture of artefacts allows them to use traditional skills and locally available materials to earn money. Items are produced on a casual or 'piece rate' basis, which allows people to make items in their own time, free from the constraints of the formal labour market. It also leaves time to pursue other important cultural and economic activities such as attending ceremonies, 'looking after' the country and hunting, fishing and gathering.

Of particular significance is the direct correlation between accruing social status and prestige and producing items for sale. The manufacture of artefacts is, in part, based on individual creativity and skill, but it is also based, in many cases, on the access to 'inside' knowledge about religious life. Consequently, producers who are successful are frequently making a statement about their status within Aboriginal society. An additional benefit is that they can gain a reputation in the wider community as successful artists and this adds to their secular status. While returns to artists can include substantial non-monetary returns (like social status), it is imperative to recognise that Aboriginal people produce *for the market* primarily for financial reasons.

Finally, the manufacture of artefacts is an area where Aboriginal people have a unique, comparative advantage and virtual monopoly. In other words, there is no one else who can produce *genuine* Aboriginal artefacts the way Aboriginal people themselves produce them.

The marketing system

To convert their unique, comparative advantage in the production of artefacts into economic gain, Aboriginal people must first find a market niche. This in turn is dependent on an effective marketing system.

The fact that the overall economic significance of artefact manufacture for producers is limited can be interpreted in a number of ways. One possibility is that the market grossly undervalues commercialised Aboriginal material culture. This may be hard for many buyers of Aboriginal art to believe because quality artefacts are not cheap in galleries in capital cities. Another possibility is that there are inefficiencies in the marketing of Aboriginal art that result in the producer receiving a fraction of the final price. A third possibility is that complexities in the current industry structure undermine the potential for fair returns to producers.

Features of the industry

A number of broad industry features complicate the marketing of Aboriginal art. Firstly, Aboriginal artefacts are highly variable, – in size, in quality and in type (they may be traditional, derivative, or modern). This in turn means that they are earmarked for very different market segments ranging from tourist art to collectors' art. Which segment an artefact may fit into is influenced not only by its type and quality, but also by its retail price and the way it is marketed. As with all art, there is a great deal of subjectivity in this process. With Aboriginal art this is frequently amplified because items are sold at outlets in state capital cities that are remote from the producers. Consequently, the seller is frequently unaware of the cultural significance of an item, but sells it primarily on an assessment of its aesthetic worth that is itself frequently influenced by its wholesale price.

The major problem is in the way the industry is structured. Most producers are not only remote from markets, but are not involved in the wholesaling or retailing of artefacts. Producers frequently live at remote locations and in small outstation communities, isolated from each other. This has meant that, until recently, artists have been unable to form an effective pressure group to represent their interests. In general, community craft centres employ craft advisers who are responsible for collecting artefacts from a region and acting as agents for the artists.

The proportion of the final price the producer receives for an item is directly linked to the geographic location of final retail outlets. Hence artefacts sold at Uluru National Park return artists about 60 per cent of final price, whereas artefacts sold at a private gallery in Sydney or Melbourne may return the artists as little as 15 to 30 per cent of final price. This proportion is largely dependent on the number of intermediaries involved in the marketing process. While the actual amount that a producer receives may not reflect this disparity, the potential for maximising returns to producers is linked to marketing items as near as possible to the point of manufacture.

Government subvention of art marketing

It is partly because of these complexities that there has been a high degree of government intervention in the marketing of Aboriginal art in the last two decades.

The artefact industry has had a short and somewhat chequered history. A 1965 report on the Australian tourism industry emphasised the need for an effective marketing authority. In 1971, the then Office of Aboriginal Affairs established Aboriginal Arts and Crafts Pty Ltd as a Sydney-based company to both wholesale and retail Aboriginal artefacts. In 1973, the Aboriginal Arts Board (AAB) of the Australian Council was established. The AAB has progressively funded an increasing number of community craft centres since then and these centres have become an integral component of the industry. From 1976 to 1984, the AAB also funded Aboriginal Arts and Crafts Pty Ltd. This arrangement altered in 1984 when another company called Inada Holdings, funded by the Aboriginal Development Commission (ADC), took over the role of Aboriginal Arts and Crafts Pty Ltd. Inada Holdings is now called Aboriginal Arts Australia (AAA).

For the past decade government support for the Aboriginal artefact industry has occurred in two main ways – through community craft centres and via the marketing company. Currently all community craft centres share an amount similar to the ADC's operating subsidy to Aboriginal Arts Australia.

PLATE 24 *Workers in the print workshop at Tiwi Designs on Bathurst Island.*

Nobody challenges the fact that public sector intervention was both justified and required in the early 1970s when Aboriginal art was a relatively unknown artistic tradition. But in recent years, the popularity of Aboriginal art has increased to such an extent that it is well known among both Australian and international art buyers and among tourists. In the past two or three years there has been an unprecedented increase in private sector involvement in the marketing of Aboriginal art. This has meant that the company has acted less and less as a marketing authority (usually regarded as a statutory marketing monopoly) and increasingly as just another specialist retailer. This calls into question the role of publicly funded Aboriginal art galleries, particularly in southern cities where private galleries abound.

In recent years, federal government policy in Aboriginal affairs has stressed the need for economic equality between Aboriginal and non-Aboriginal Australians based on the principle of employment equity. Both the Miller and the Blanchard Homeland Reports noted that at many Aboriginal communities this goal will only be achieved by supporting such industries as the manufacture of artefacts. Hence while government support for the industry appears assured in the immediate future, policy makers will want to ensure that public money spent in subsidising this industry will result in increased income and improved economic status for producers.

Tensions in the industry

A problematic feature of the artefact industry is that the majority of artists live in the north of Australia while AAA's head office is in Sydney. In 1987 the artists formed the Association of Northern and Central Australian Aboriginal Artists (ANCAAA) to directly represent their interests. This association's membership includes the majority of Aboriginal artists in Australia. Its aim is to have overall independence and, specifically, autonomy from the southern-based Aboriginal Arts Australia. The catalyst for the establishment of the association was a proposal by the then Minister for Aboriginal Affairs in 1987 that AAA was to have a greater role in the marketing of Aboriginal art and in the funding of community craft centres. The Minister's aim was that returns to artists should be increased by such industry restructuring; it was implied that inefficiencies in the industry occurred at community craft centres. With hindsight, it now seems that conflict between crafts people and the government-backed marketing company was inevitable and that the Minister's statement merely hastened this development.

During 1987, the community craft centres that were members of ANCAAA moved to boycott sales to AAA. There were political, economic and cultural reasons for the dispute. Artists and their representatives believed that the artefact industry was in danger of being increasingly dominated by southern

Aboriginal and non-Aboriginal interests with the proposed restructuring. This shift in control was politically unacceptable to them. They also believed that the marketing role should occur geographically closer to, and under the direct control of the producers, in order to maximise their financial returns. Culturally, there was a real fear that centralisation of power with AAA would unduly influence what is ordered, sold in the market and ultimately produced. In short, producers and their advisers were concerned that the cultural integrity of items produced would be undermined. Though to some extent craft advisers themselves influence what is produced (on the basis of market signals, personal tastes and local alliances), the Aboriginal communities that employ them are at liberty to sack them. There can be no such direct accountability with a Sydney-based company.

While it is undeniable that the artefact manufacturing industry requires financial aid, this should be provided in a relatively value-neutral manner. Social security entitlements to most producers may be seen as providing this kind of aid; this is value-neutral because it is paid to people as a minimum income irrespective of what is produced. Social security could be regarded as a production subsidy, except that producers receive these payments as a civil right as Australian citizens. The complex nature of the industry means that government assistance is necessary to ensure the marketing of artefacts.

Recent developments and future directions

The disagreement between ANCAAA and AAA has by now been resolved. Nevertheless, the areas of conflict outlined above identify numerous issues that have no simple answers. Three specific future issues need to be addressed. Firstly, how can impetus be given to the marketing of Aboriginal art near the location of producers? Secondly, does the marketing system need restructuring? And finally, what flow-on benefits could accrue to Aboriginal communities from artefact manufacture?

Cultural centres and art

In recent years there has been an unprecedented growth in international and domestic tourism to the north of Australia, particularly to the Northern Territory and the Kimberley region of Western Australia. Both these regions are being aggressively marketed as locations where tourists can experience Aboriginal culture.

Tourists increasingly are being given a glimpse of the Aboriginal way of life by Aboriginal-led tours to places like Ipolera (near Gosse's Bluff in central Australia), Bamurru Djadjam (Goose Camp) in Kakadu National Park and at Putjamirra on Melville Island. However, only a fraction of all tourists have the opportunity to visit these places.

Since the early 1980s it has been recognised that there is a need for cultural centres at places like Kakadu, Uluru and Katherine Gorge National Parks. The Northern Territory Government has plans to establish a cultural centre near Darwin, but funding for other centres has not been forthcoming. It has always been envisaged that these locations would not only provide displays about traditional and contemporary Aboriginal culture, but that they would emphasise both the manufacture and sale of material culture.

The only example of a cultural centre that is currently operating is a craft camp (*Punu Ngurra*) established at Uluru National Park in early 1986. It consists of a number of traditional shelters and windbreaks where Pitjantjatjara people demonstrate their manufacturing skills to tourists and a wide range of artefacts are available for sale. This is currently the most successful community craft outlet in Australia and provides a model for other Aboriginal communities near important tourist destinations.

Cultural centres have two potential advantages as marketing outlets. Firstly, they could provide a means to emphasise the cultural context of Aboriginal art and craft as well as its aesthetic merits. Secondly, they could be established at locations with high visitor numbers. This would mean that tourists would have the opportunity to procure items directly from community craft enterprises, thus ensuring that producers received a higher proportion of the final price and higher returns.

Restructuring the marketing system

It must be recognised that it is not always possible to take the people to the culture; it will always be necessary to take some of the culture to the people. This is particularly so in the Aboriginal artefact industry because of its diversity; there will always be a range of items that will be procured by museums and collectors rather than tourists.

There has been a recent increase in the number of private sector outlets marketing Aboriginal artefacts. This in itself does not ensure that Aboriginal producers' rights are protected, but communities are starting to learn about standard markups in the 'art industry' and are in a stronger bargaining position to insist on fair treatment from galleries as overall demand for Aboriginal art expands. Community craft centres are starting to show that they can not only arrange for the collection and documentation of artefacts, but that they can also market them.

The increasingly direct link between community craft centres and final consumers means that once again producers are receiving a higher proportion of the final price. This in turn implies that the 'watchdog' role as a market leader that Aboriginal Arts and Crafts Pty Ltd and then Aboriginal Arts Australia have sought to provide may no longer be required.

There are indications that the industry now has somewhat different requirements. The new needs are for an Aboriginal-controlled organisation, based in northern Australia, that acts as a resource organisation on behalf of all the Aboriginal craft centres. This resource organisation could train Aboriginal people to work in the industry. It could produce exhibition catalogues and documentation and help co-ordinate community craft centres in joint exhibitions in southern and northern galleries, and assist in the delivery of stock to retail outlets (cultural centres) in the north. To some extent, ANCAAA has already fulfilled this role over the past year. It has a corporate structure that ensures direct accountability to community craft centres and, through them, to producers. The implication of ANCAAA's emergence is that there may now be a need for the allocation of government funding to this new organisation.

Channelling the spinoffs to Aboriginal communities

To maximise returns to producers so as to ensure the future supply of artefacts, and to establish employment equity between Aboriginal and other Australians, it will be necessary to establish links between the artefact manufacturing sector and the wider economy at Aboriginal communities.

To date, most of the income and associated spinoffs from artefact manufacture have gone to people outside the producers' communities. Some of these benefits could be enjoyed within Aboriginal communities if Aboriginal people were more directly involved in retailing artefacts. A likely possibility here, is to employ Aboriginal people at cultural centres. This currently occurs at Uluru National Park. There are also employment possibilities for Aboriginal people in poster production and catalogue publication and a potential for expansion into textile and graphic design and the manufacture of clothing. It is not suggested that such opportunities will emerge overnight; there may be a need for training programs to provide Aboriginal people with the requisite skills for such employment.

What is important is that the currently embryonic artefact-manufacturing sector currently provides the main goods for export from Aboriginal communities in northern Australia. Any growth in this export industry must provide a stimulus to Aboriginal regional economies and Aboriginal businesses. This will only occur if the emphasis on the marketing of artefacts in north Australia is increased.

Conclusion: the future survival of Aboriginal art

More and more Australians are buying Aboriginal art; it is almost mandatory to buy something Australian in 1988 and what could be more Australian than an Aboriginal painting or artefact. The current boom in the industry augurs well for the immediate viability of the Aboriginal artefact industry. In terms of its future, the Aboriginal artefacts industry is at an important cross-road and considerable and thoughtful attention must be given to restructuring this industry. The industry's strength is in northern and central Australia where more and more Australian and overseas tourists are visiting. There may be a need to shift the marketing emphasis to this part of Australia to increase returns to artists, and to maximise economic spinoffs to Aboriginal communities, the tourism industry and the northern economy. There are also important cultural reasons for pursuing this strategy, linked to the maintenance of the cultural integrity of artefacts produced and sold.

Despite the current popularity of Aboriginal art, without a firmer economic base there will be no industry in the long run. This does not mean that Aboriginal culture for Aboriginal people will either be radically transformed or will decline. Rather, the consequences will be felt by non-Aboriginal people whose primary access to Aboriginal culture is via the procurement of material culture. To return to the title of the radio program mentioned earlier, without artists there *may* be no culture, but without reasonable financial returns, there *will* be no artists and no artefacts for sale.

JON ALTMAN

The Economic Domain

Artists in the Northern Territory often draw upon the everyday economic themes of hunting and gathering, or the plants and animals of the environment for their paintings. Perhaps nowhere is this better expressed than in the art of western Arnhem Land. Here the hunter's detailed knowledge of anatomy is succinctly and imaginatively captured in the x-ray style of painting, where the internal organs and skeletal details of the animals are depicted. Economic themes are also extended into introduced media, such as the canvas paintings from central Australia and the delicate batik silks with their interpretative designs of familiar plants and animals.

PLATE 25
George Milpurrurru
Maningrida/NT
Hunting scene 1975
Ochre on bark
98 x 71.2cm irreg
Ganalbuyngu Language Group
Gurrumba Gurrumba Clan
Yirritja Moiety

This painting depicts a kangaroo being speared by a hunter, shown at the lower right of the kangaroo. There are numerous carved, pronged, fighting spears shown amongst the figures. A spearthrower, several boomerangs and some stone axes are depicted below the kangaroo. In the top left corner are the flames of the hunters' campfire. Dismembered portions of the cooked kangaroo are also shown near the animal's stomach and tail.

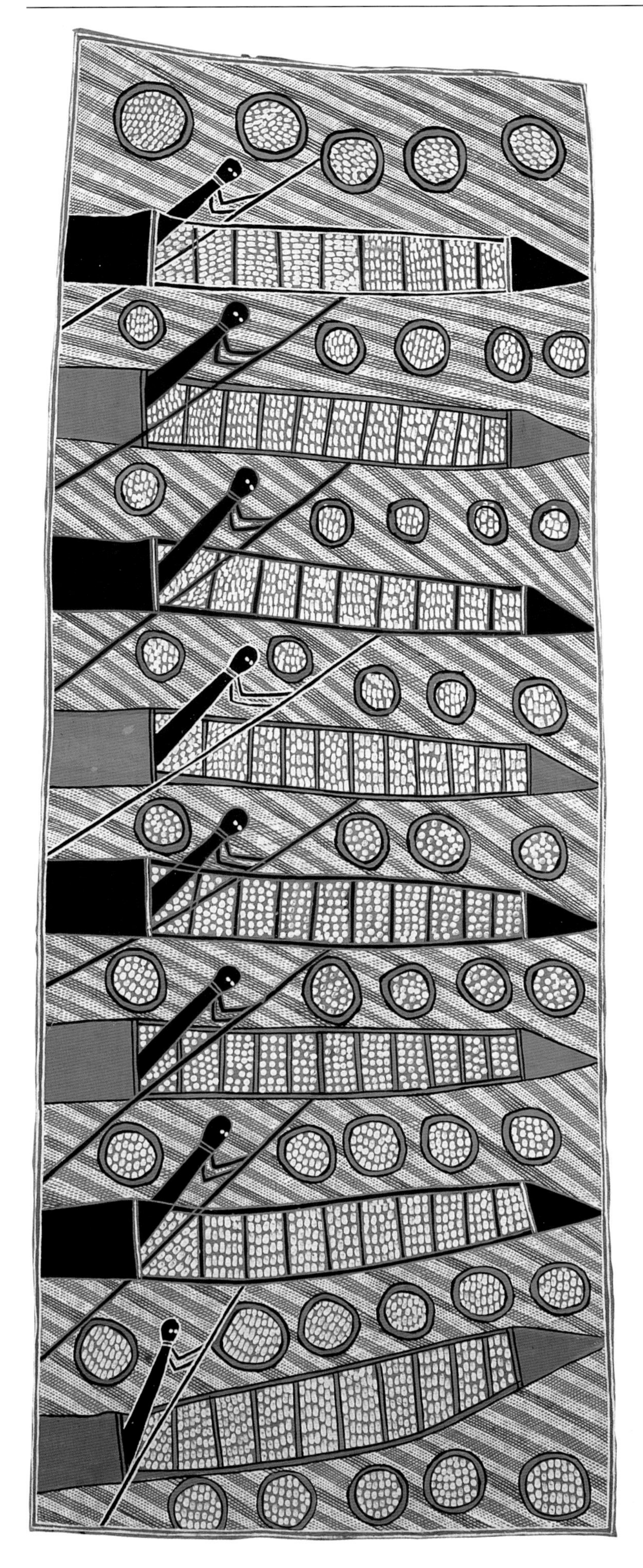

PLATE 26
George Milpurrurru
Ramingining/NT
Goose hunting in the Arafura Swamp 1987
Ochre on bark
157.5 x 60cm irreg
Ganalbuyngu Language Group
Gurrumba Gurrumba Clan
Yirritja Moiety

*In the Arafura Swamp region of central Arnhem Land, the people relied upon resources such as the magpie goose (*Anseranus semipalmata*) and its eggs, which are abundant during the wet season. This painting depicts the goose-hunters poling through the swamp in their flat-bottomed bark canoes gathering goose eggs, which are represented by the small white ovals. The eggs in their circular nests are also depicted.*

PLATE 27
George Milpurrurru
Ramingining/NT
Pythons with their eggs 1986
Ochre on bark
141.7 x 51.5cm irreg
Ganalbuyngu Language Group
Gurrumba Gurrumba Clan
Yirritja Moiety

The black-headed python is one of the artist's totems. The style is typical of painting in central Arnhem Land where figures are depicted with complex background and internal patterns.

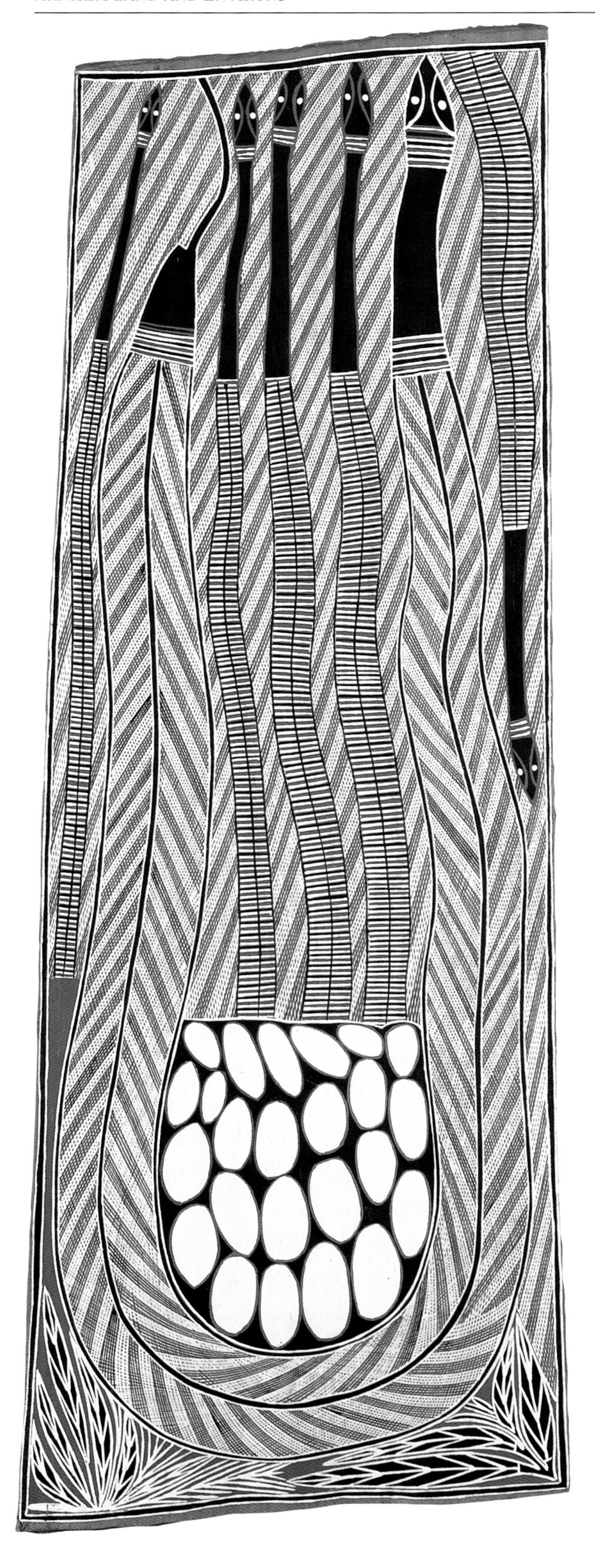

PLATE 28
Nandabitta
Groote Eylandt/NT
Fishing scene 1969
Ochre on bark
59 x 39.2cm irreg
Anindilyakwa Language Group

A fishing scene in the Gulf of Carpentaria, close to Groote Eylandt, is shown in this painting. A fisherman, in a canoe, can be seen spearfishing a manta ray. Also depicted are various forms of marine game, such as sting ray and sawfish. On the bank, a man is singing to the rhythm of his clap-sticks to aid the hunt.

PLATE 29
Lofty Nabarrayal
Oenpelli/NT
Butchering scene 1970
Ochre on bark
58.5 x 44.4cm irreg
Kunwinjku/Dangbon Language Group
Mok Clan

After a successful hunt, a man and his wife butcher a kangaroo. They are depicted back at their camp, with the hindquarters and arm of the dismembered kangaroo. Below them is their bark shelter on its frame of wooden saplings. To the left is the man's spear and spearthrower; to the right of the shelter is the woman's dillybag and axe. According to the Kunwinjku group, Aboriginal people did not know how to cut up a kangaroo until they saw mimi *spirits doing it. The* mimi *spirits removed the hands, feet and the head, separating each leg, then the back, the chest, the shoulders, the tail and lastly the hindquarters of the kangaroo. Often the internal bars that divide the sections of an x-ray style painting of an animal are indicators of how the animal should be butchered.*

PLATE 30
Peter Maralwanga (deceased)
Maragalidban/NT
Namanggol, the barramundi 1980
Ochre on bark
53.7 x 132.5cm irreg
Kunwinjku Language Group
Nagardbam Clan

*With the formation of an estuarine environment in western Arnhem Land after the last Ice Age, some 8,000 years ago, fish such as the barramundi became an important source of food. Images of barramundi (*Lates calcarifer*) proliferate in the rock art galleries of the escarpment region, as well as in the bark paintings from that area. The barramundi is a Yirritja moiety totem associated with the formation of the East Alligator River. The x-ray style of the painting characterises the art of western Arnhem Land. It is typified by the portrayal of the animal's skeleton and internal organs.*

PLATE 31
Wally Mandarrk (deceased)
Korlobirrahda/NT
Ngohnghoh, the rock pandanus 1979
Ochre on bark
95.5 x 41cm irreg
Gune/Dangbon Language Group
Barabba Clan

Ngohnghoh, the rock pandanus (Pandanus basedowi), *grows in the rocky escarpment country of Arnhem Land. Like other species of pandanus endemic to the Top End, it produces large clusters of fruit which are ready to drop in the late dry season. The bases of the segments may be chewed and sucked raw, or soaked in water before eating. The fallen segments are more often gathered and cut transversely to allow the small nuts inside to be extracted with a sharpened stick or piece of wire. Ngohnghoh is said to be an inferior food to other pandanus species as it has a bitter taste. The* mimi *spirits of the rock country, however, consider it good tucker. Pandanus plants growing along watercourses are described as belonging to a Yirritja moiety, while those growing in desert places are regarded as a Dua moiety species.*

PLATE 32
Wally Mandarrk (deceased)
Korlobirrahda/NT
Waiyara spirit from Benebenemdi 1979
Ochre on bark
91 x 40cm irreg
Gune/Dangbon
Language Group
Barabba Clan

The Waiyara Spirit is associated with mandjanek, *which is also called the 'cheeky' yam. This is because it is a slightly toxic and bitter tasting yam which is made edible by leaching. In this painting the Spirit is depicted carrying two kinds of dillybag. The one on the left is known as* bulbbe *and it is tightly woven for carrying wild honey. The other dillybag on the right is called* dangke *and it has a loose weave which is suitable for collecting the* mandjanek *yams, and for soaking them in running water.*

PLATE 33
Dick Nguleingulei Murrumurru
Kukadjerri/NT
Two kangaroos 1980
Ochre on bark
96 x 67.8cm irreg
Kunwinjku Language Group
Nawakadji Subsection
Nabularlhdja Clan

Kangaroos are a favourite flesh food amongst Aboriginal people. The depiction of these animals, with their internal organs represented in the well known x-ray style, indicates that they are just 'tucker' animals, as opposed to Ancestral Beings, who would be distinguished by cross-hatched, internal detailing.

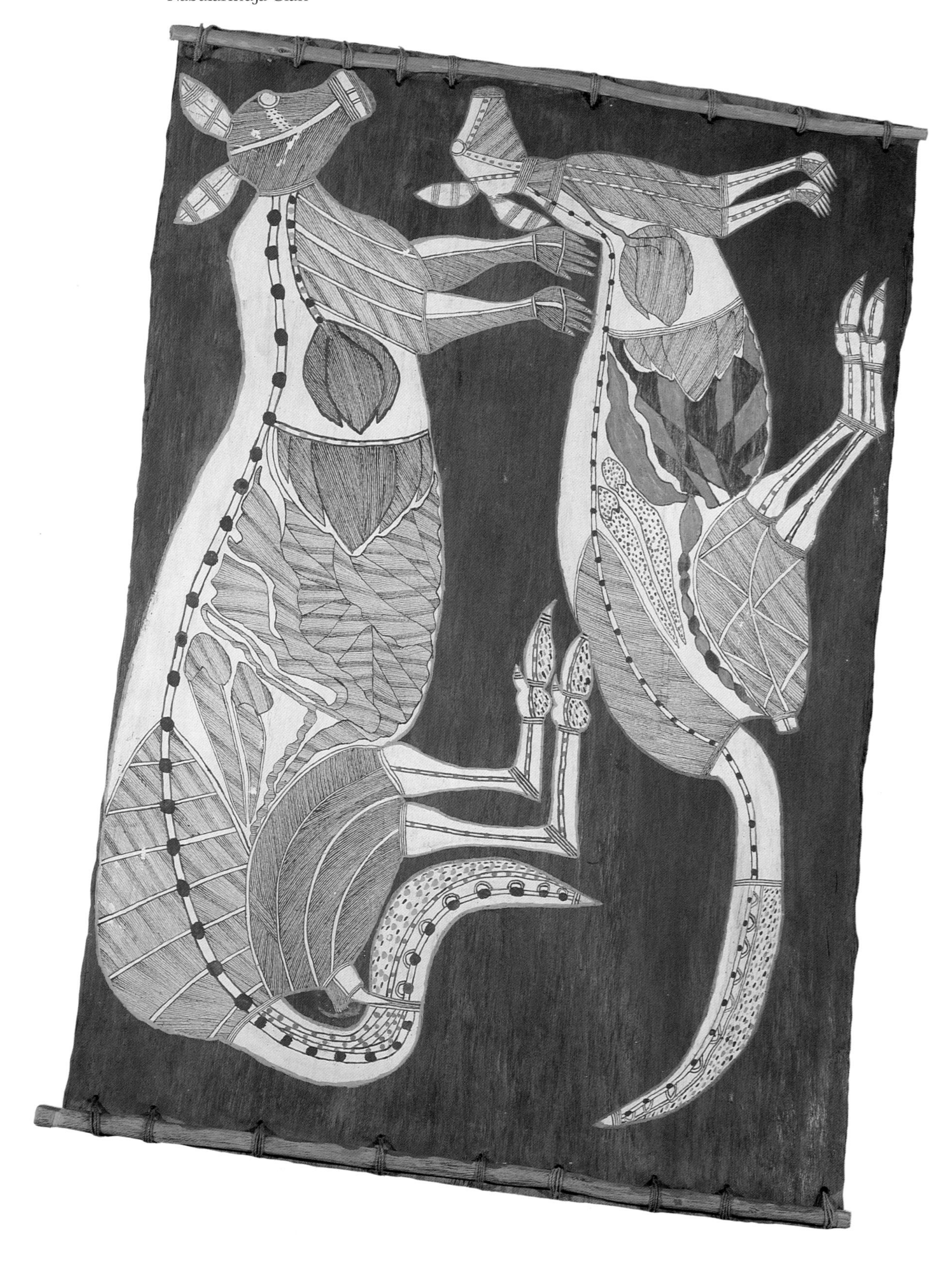

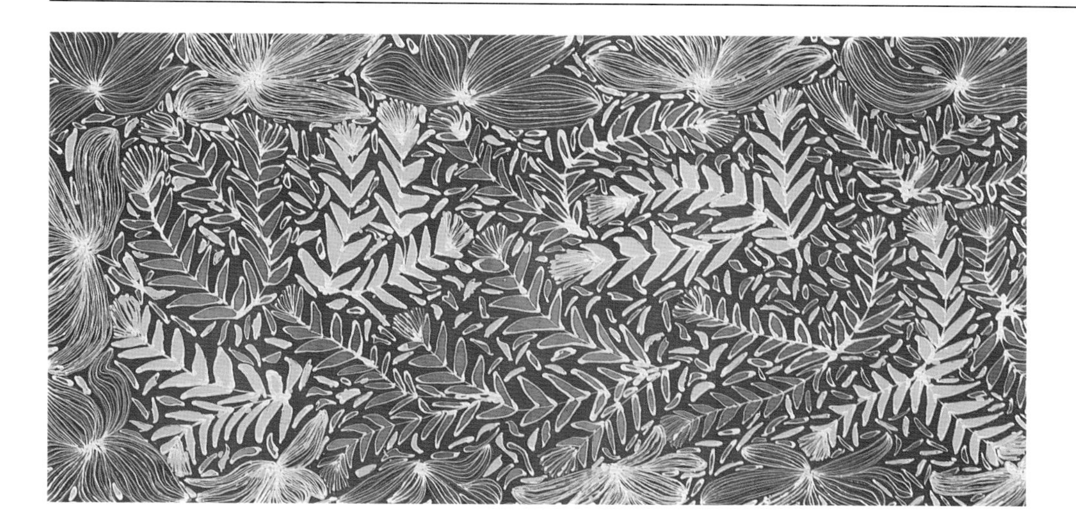

PLATE 34
Gloria Ngala
Utopia Station/NT
Floral design 1987
Batik on silk
111 x 221.2cm
Anmatyerre
Language Group

Women usually depict the plants of their environment, especially the bush foods that they gather. There was no information given about the plant species illustrated in this batik.

PLATE 35
Gloria Ngala
Utopia Station/NT
Floral design 1987
Batik on silk
116.7 x 169.2cm
Anmatyerre
Language Group

This batik is a floral design with lizards, insects, caterpillars and echidnas.

PLATE 36
Angkuna Graham
Ernabella/SA
Abstract design 1987
Batik on silk
112 x 202.2cm
Pitjantjatjara
Language Group

This form of decoration was invented by the Pitjantjatjara women and is based on the flora of their environment. It is a style which they all use, even though it has no traditional origin.

The Religious Domain

The majority of Aboriginal art is religious. In the graphic arts, most paintings depict the mythology of the Dreamtime, although the way the myths are portrayed varies from region to region. The numerous styles reflect the broad cultural differences among the Northern Territory groups of Melville and Bathurst Islands, western and north-eastern Arnhem Land, Groote Eylandt and central Australia. However, while these regional styles vary from naturalistic to abstract, the messages are similar.

Most paintings portray the powerful Ancestral Beings of the Dreamtime, the journeys that they undertook and the places where they performed certain acts. Many paintings also illustrate the rituals that the Ancestral Beings instigated and the ritual objects that they created. Such ceremonial themes vary according to regional practice. So for example in the arid centre, paintings often relate to ceremonies concerned with increasing the productivity of the land. On the other hand, mortuary ceremonies are extremely important in Arnhem Land and the adjacent Melville and Bathurst Islands, and this is reflected in their paintings and carvings.

Apart from the Ancestral Beings, there are many less important Spirit Beings who are believed to inhabit particular sites. Belief in Spirit Beings is particularly wide-spread in western Arnhem Land, providing the artists with another facet of the religious domain for illustration.

PLATE 37
Johnny Bulun Bulun
Gamedi/near Maningrida/NT
Mortuary story 1982
Ochre on bark
111 x 97.1cm irreg
Ganalbuyngu Language Group
Gurumba Gurumba Clan
Yirritja Moiety

The painting depicts the final stage of a mortuary ceremony when the stripped bones of the deceased are broken and placed into a hollow log bone-pole (depicted in the centre of the painting). At the top of the pole, one of the deceased's male relatives is placing the skull into the bone-pole. The rest of the bones are shown in the top right hand corner of the painting. On either side are the mourners.

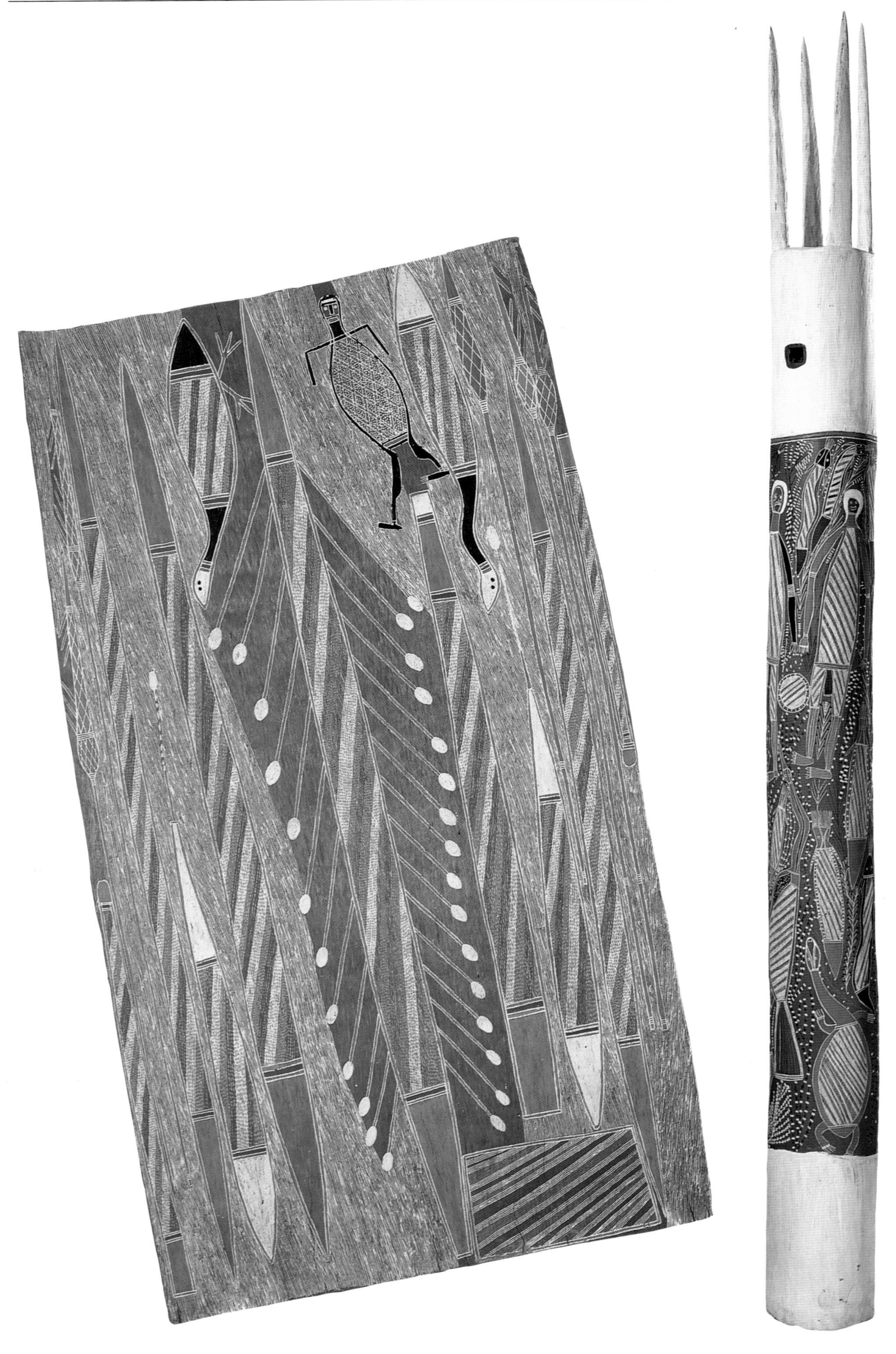

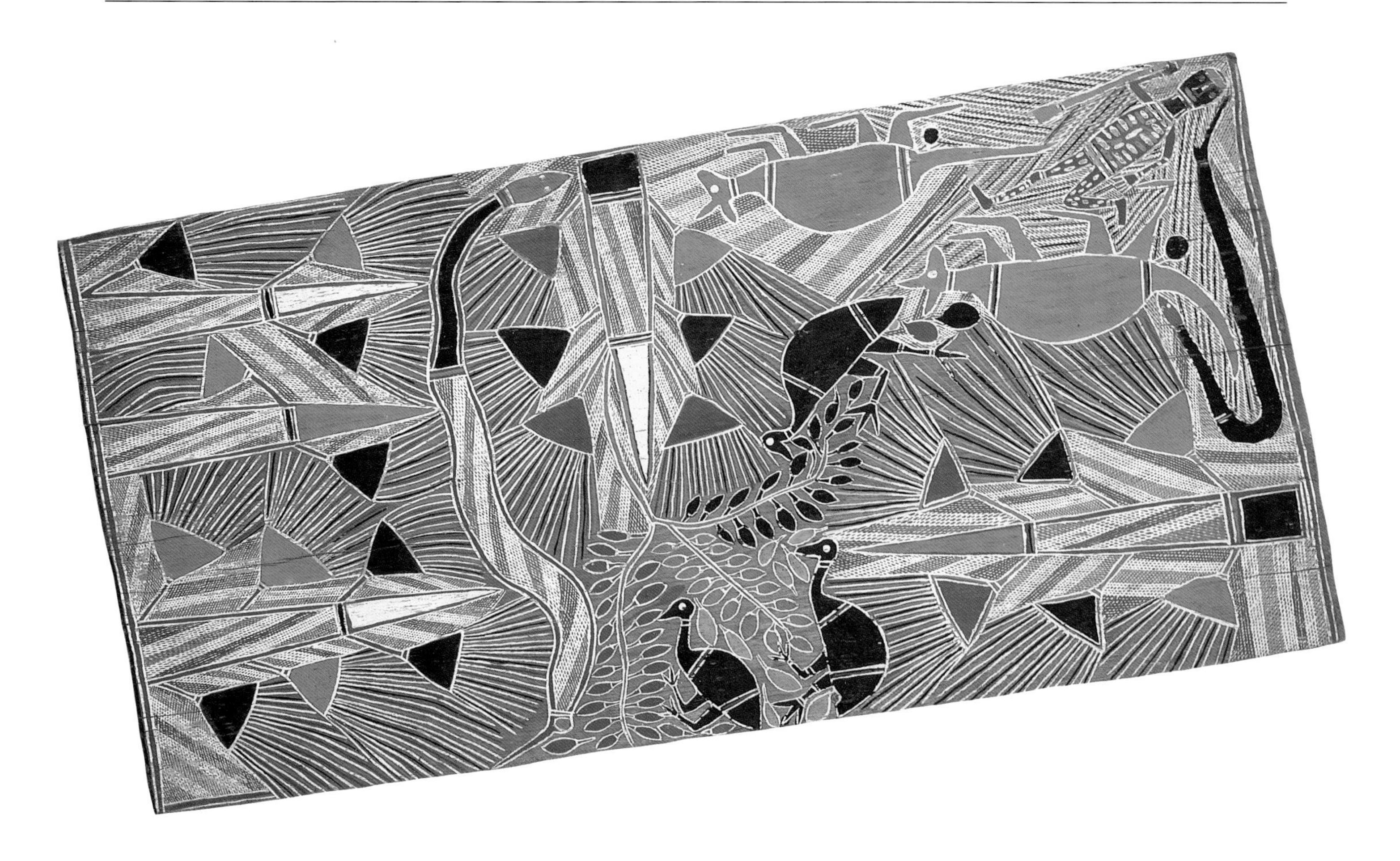

PLATE 38
Lipundja 1 (deceased)
Milingimbi/NT
Murryana 1984
Ochre on bark
154.3 x 84.5cm irreg
Gupapuyngu Language Group
Daygurrgurr Clan
Yirritja Moiety

In the Dreamtime, Murryana was responsible for introducing the hollow log mortuary ceremony to the Gupapuyngu people. This painting depicts him painted with a totemic 'sugar bag' design of interlocked diamonds. Murryana is directly above a paperbark rangga *which is his representation. On either side are the bullroarers which are twirled by the men during the final dance at a mortuary ceremony. These symbolise the way in which the deceased's soul is caught by diver birds, in the same way that the birds catch freshwater fish. Also included in the painting are: a paperbark emu* rangga *(sacred mortuary sculpture), a Morning Star pole and the clan waterhole to which the deceased's soul will return.*

PLATE 39
Ngalabya
Hollow log coffin 1982
Gartji/NT
Ochre on wood
137.2 x 20.1 x 19cm
Djinang Language Group
Djalawurrwurr Clan

Djam-murmur is the hollow log coffin of the Yirritja Djalawurrwurr clan whose territory centres on Gartji waterhole, west of Ramingining. The holes on either side are the eyes of the log coffin. Except for two human figures, the designs depict totems which the Djalawurrwurr share with other Yirritja clans of the east and west. The figures, according to the artist, are those of real men whose names were Bamadulpa and Djarmilmera. These elders taught the artist the stories associated with totems. Under the hands of the two figures are circular cross-hatched designs, representing the Gartji waterhole. The other totems are diving birds, the long-necked tortoise, water snake and eel-tailed cat-fish.

PLATE 40
Bininuewuy (deceased)
Milingimbi/NT 1928-1983
The waterhole by the palm trees
c. 1970
Ochre on bark
128.7 x 67.4cm irreg
Djambarrpuyngu Language Group
Ngaladhar Clan
Dhuwa Moiety

Some of the subjects of songs and dances from Djambarrpuyngu mortuary ceremonies are represented in this painting. These ceremonies are mainly concerned with the flora and fauna in and around a sacred waterhole which is surrounded by cabbage tree palms. The large carpet snake in the grass (cross-hatched background) is found here, along with the large kangaroos which are hunted by Aboriginal people. Other small birds and snakes live in the branches of the cabbage tree palms.

PLATE 41
Lipundja 1 (deceased)
Milingimbi/NT
Mortuary painting 1967
Ochre on bark
125 x 53.5cm irreg
Gupapuyngu Language Group
Daygurrgurr Clan
Yirritja Moiety

This painting shows the Gupapuyngu people's hollow log coffin (djalumbu) *and the bones of the deceased. The log has two eyes so that the Spirit can see the ceremony and come out for food. The upper leg bones are shown on the upper and lower edge of the painting. The curved bones are the ribs. The four bones close to the coffin are the lower leg bones, the tibia and the fibula, with the arm bones and attached hands positioned on the edge. One hand has a finger missing, as it was removed from the corpse and kept by relatives. The gourd shapes are shoulder blades and the skulls are shown with the deceased's totemic pattern. The two leaf shapes, on a string to the left, are the 'sorcery sickness' which has caused his death by transferring sickness along the string into the victim's bones.*

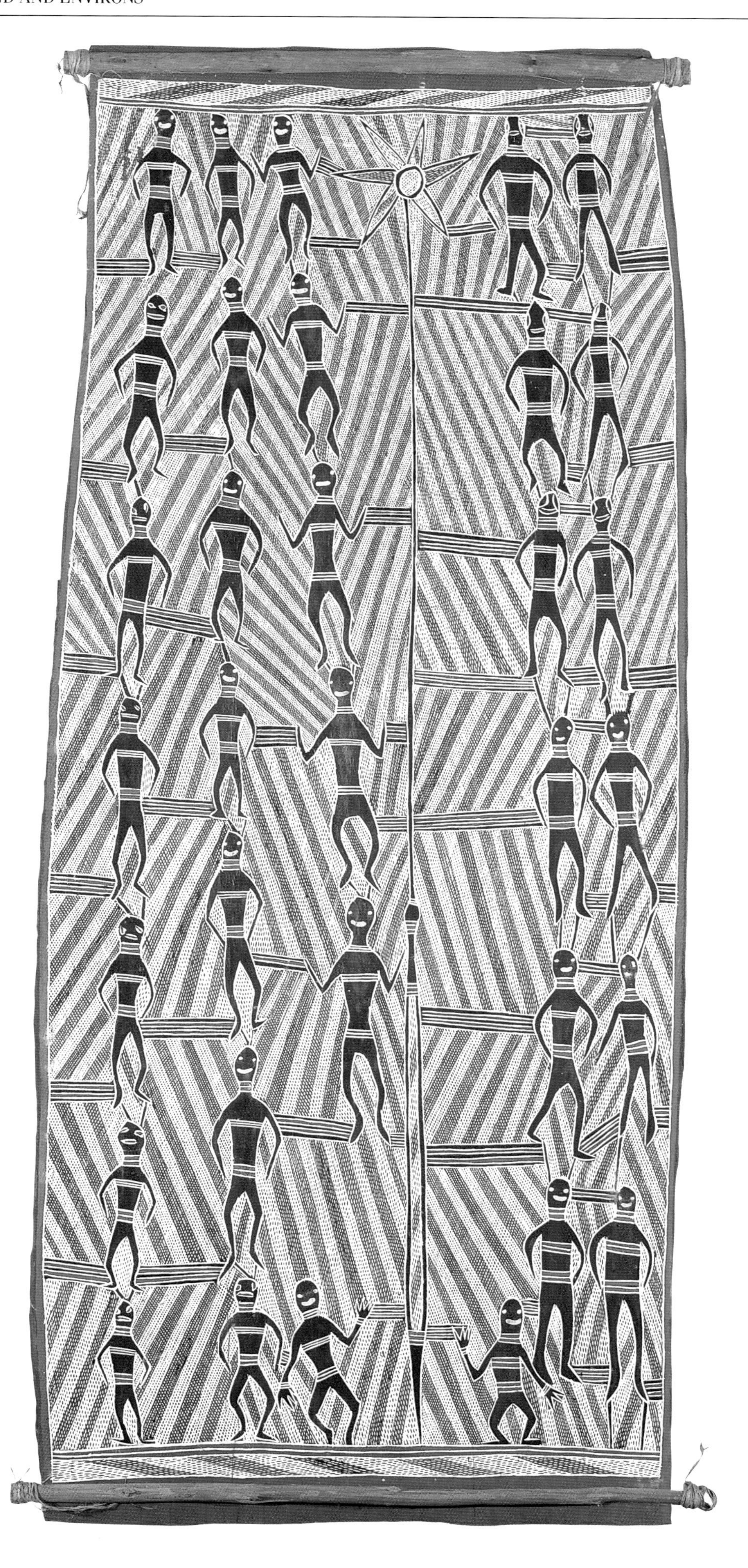

PLATE 42
Manjuwi
Galiwinku/Elcho Island/NT
Wulumumu, Morning Star story 1981
Ochre on bark
157.5 x 70.7cm irreg
Gurruwirri Language Group
Galpu Clan
Dhuwa Moiety

The Ancestral Being, Wulumumu has a Dreaming place at Garulu. Here Wulumumu hunted sting-rays and gathered yams which he placed in his dillybag. He is associated with Barnumbirr, the Morning Star. During mortuary ceremonies the deceased's soul is said to be guided to the Land of the Dead by a feathered string connected to the Morning Star, as illustrated in this bark painting. At the base of the painting people are performing a mortuary ceremony. In the centre is a Morning Star pole, surmounted by Barnumbirr, the Morning Star. The two bark paintings, the carving and two Morning Star poles belong to a set which illustrates the Morning Star story.

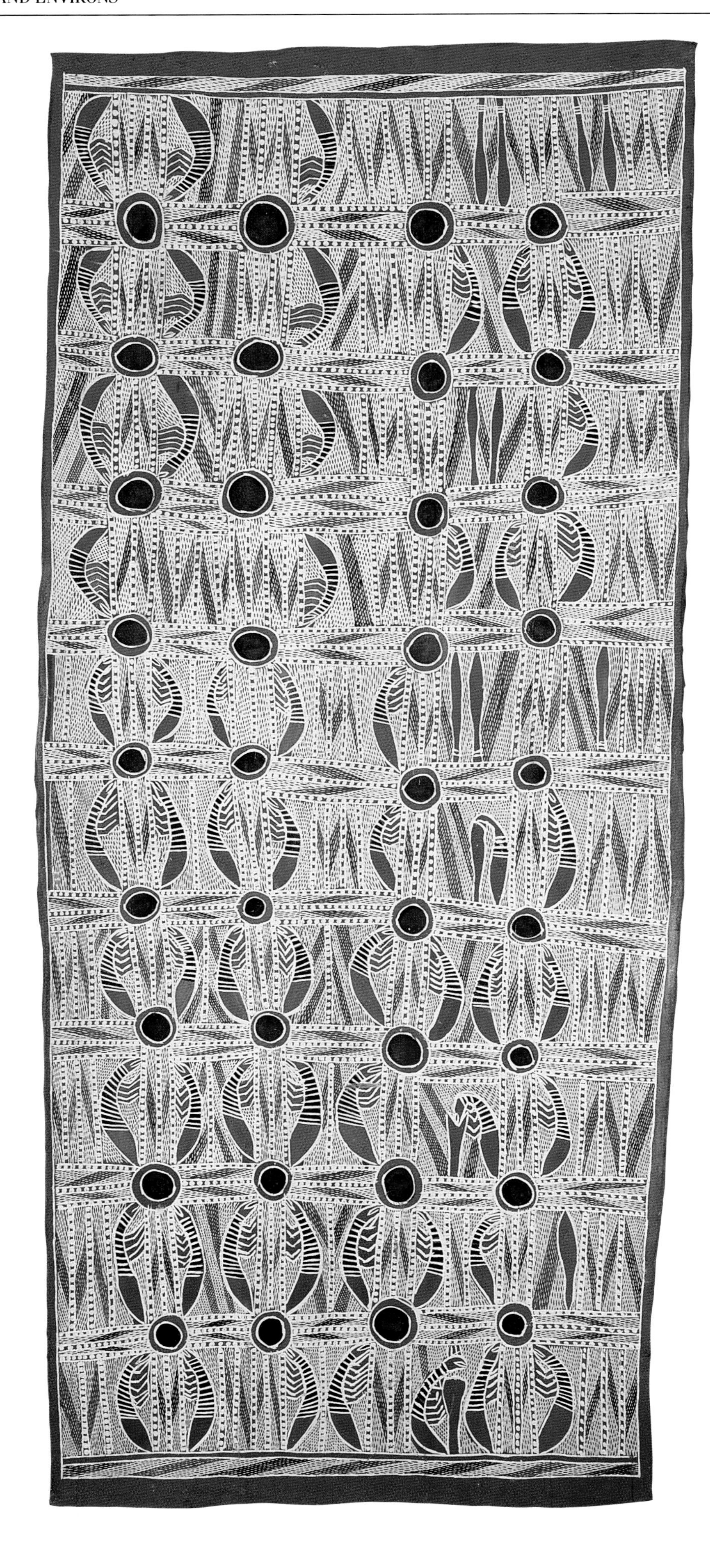

PLATE 43
Manjuwi
Galiwinku/Elcho Island/NT
Wurrkadi 1981
Ochre on bark
154.5 x 70.3cm irreg
Gurruwirri Language Group
Galpu Clan
Dhuwa Moiety

This bark painting depicts tiny animals called Wurrkadi, *who live in small holes on the beach. The lines with white dots are their tracks in the sand and the black circles are their homes. The white cross-hatching represents the remains of the yam,* gulaka, *upon which they have been feeding. The yellow and black hatchings represent the grooves made upon the beach by the rain or the tide. On another level these* Wurrkadi *represent people performing the cleansing of a mortuary ceremony. The analogy here is with the small* Wurrkadi *crustacea who keep the beach clean by disposing of any debris, which the mourners leave buried in the sand sculpture made on the beach for the ritual.*

PLATE 44
Charlie Gunbuna
Maningrida/NT
Mortuary story 1975
Ochre on bark
71 x 32.9cm irreg
Djinang Language Group
Urgiganjdjar Clan
Dhuwa Moiety

Illustrating the final stages of the Djinang mortuary ceremony, the figures are dancing the moykuy *spirit dance. The yellow background indicates the dust rising from the ground as they dance. The black indicates it is night time. The white lines linking the stars with the figures in the lower part represent the strings by which the Morning Star is linked to Bralgu, the Land of the Dead. In this way the Morning Star guides a person's soul to its final resting place. In the left centre panel the artist has depicted the pandanus tree which grows in the Land of the Dead. The bustard bird above, announces the arrival of a new spirit.*

PLATE 45
Left
Manjuwi
Galiwinku/Elcho Island/NT
Morning Star pole 1979
String, feathers and ochre on wood
102 x 5 x 5cm
Gurruwirri Language Group
Galpu Clan
Dhuwa Moiety

Right
Muwurra
Galiwinku/Elcho Island/NT
Morning Star pole 1980
String, feathers and ochre on wood
94 x 6 x 6cm
Datiwuy Clan
Dhuwa Moiety

Morning Star poles are ceremonial poles used by performers in a Morning Star burial ceremony. The Morning Star connects the feathered string to the deceased's soul, to guide it to the Land of the Dead.

PLATE 46
Manjuwi
Galiwinku/Elcho Island/NT
Wulumumu 1981
Fibre, string, hair, woven basket, feathers and ochre on wood
133.2 x 40 x 23cm with base
Gurruwirri Language Group
Galpu Clan
Dhuwa Moiety

Wulumumu is an Ancestral Being of the Morning Star mortuary ceremony. Barnumbirr, the Morning Star, is represented by feathered strings on Wulumumu's arms and head. This type of figurative carving is a relatively recent development. In this case, the carving was made for the sake of a collection on the theme of the Morning Star story, organised by the Museums and Art Galleries of the Northern Territory.

PLATE 47
Bede Tungatalum
Nguiu/Bathurst Island/NT
Pukumani poles with sun and stone design 1986
Synthetic polymer paint, silk-screened and hand-coloured on cotton fabric
188 x 90.7cm
Tiwi Language Group

Here the artist has combined elements from a number of silk-screen designs including the sun design and the stone design. The main feature is an artist painting a burial or Pukumani post. Posts are carved and decorated for the final stage of a mortuary ceremony and are erected around the deceased's grave as a gift from his relatives.

PLATE 48
Victor Adam (deceased)
Nguiu/Bathurst Island/NT
Pukumani burial post 1978
Ochre on ironwood
195 x 17 x 16cm
Tiwi Language Group

Pukumani burial posts, carved in ironwood and decorated with ochre designs, are placed around a grave to mark the conclusion of a mortuary ceremony. The importance of the dead person is reflected by the number and size of the posts. Often children, or perhaps old women, would have only one post, if any, while an important man might have up to twelve posts. Designs are very rarely given a derivation or mythological explanation, for they are free expressions of the artist.

PLATE 49
Unknown
Milikapiti/Melville Island/NT
Pukumani burial post 1972
Ochre on ironwood
174.3 x 22 x 21cm without base
Tiwi Language Group

PLATE 50
Unknown
Milikapiti/Melville Island/NT
Pukumani burial post 1972
Ochre on ironwood
171 x 21 x 21cm without base
Tiwi Language Group

PLATE 51
Unknown
Milikapiti/Melville Island/NT
Pukumani burial post 1972
Ochre on ironwood
137 x 27 x 27.3cm without base
Tiwi Language Group

PLATE 52
Unknown
Bathurst Island/NT
Pukumani burial post 1978
Ochre on wood
167 x 15.3 x 15cm without base
Tiwi Language Group

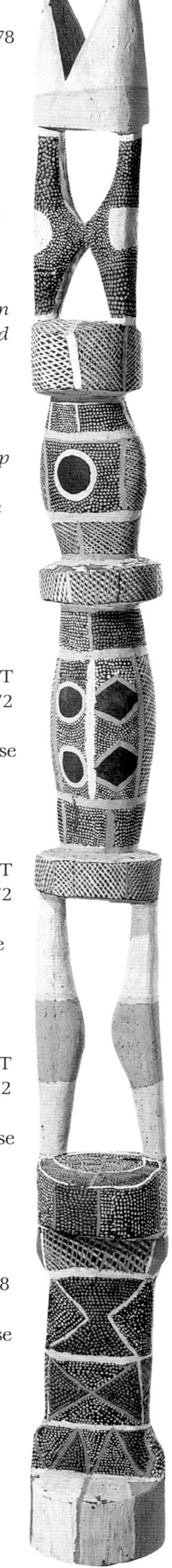

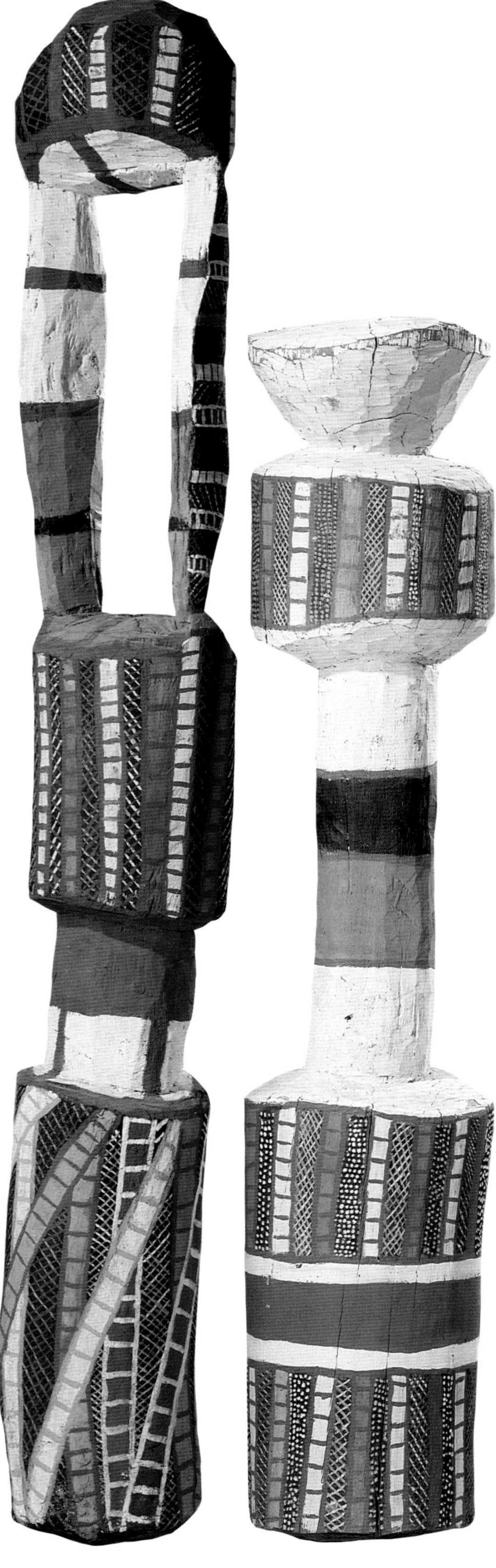

PLATE 53
Unknown
Milikapiti/Melville Island/NT
Purukuparli and Tokwampini
Ochre on wood
147.4 x 16 x 17.2cm
Tiwi Language Group

Purukuparli was the Ancestral Being who introduced death to the world. According to Tiwi mythology, Purukuparli's wife, Waijai, went out one day with their baby, Jinani, on the pretence of hunting. However she really set off to have an affair with Tapara. While she was with Tapara, she left her baby under a tree. The shade moved during the day and the baby died of exposure. Purukuparli, drawn by the cries of his wife when she had discovered her dead baby, was enraged when he discovered Jinani's death was the result of his wife's adultery. After this he decreed that all humans, who had previously been immortal, should die. He then instructed the Tiwi how to perform a burial or Pukumani ceremony with the assistance of Alikampwarni the pelican, Tangkanangki the white-breasted sea eagle, and the small bird Tokwampini.

PLATE 54
possibly David Malangi
Milingimbi/NT
Moykuy spirit c.1972
Ochre on wood
140.4 x 22 x 16.3cm without base
Liyagalawumirri Language Group
Manharrngu Clan
Dhuwa Moiety

The Yolngu of central and eastern Arnhem Land believe that a person has two souls – one is the true soul that emanates from the heart, and the other is a more shadowy and less important soul. This latter one is the moykuy *spirit, which lingers in the bush close to living Aborigines. When a person dies, the* moykuy *spirit attempts to snatch away the soul as it travels to its final resting place in the clan well.*
On the body of this moykuy *are the leaves from the trees in which it hides. Also represented are the diver bird and catfish. These are associated with mortuary ceremonies, because the diver bird catches fish in the same way as the* moykuy *tries to snatch away a person's soul.*

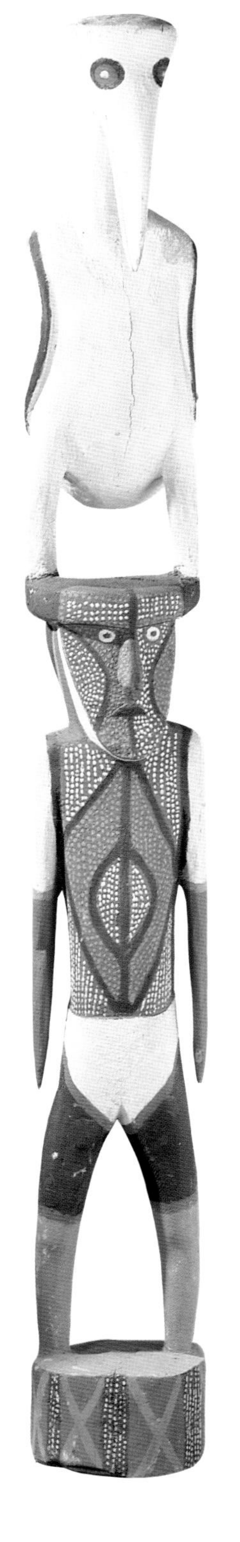

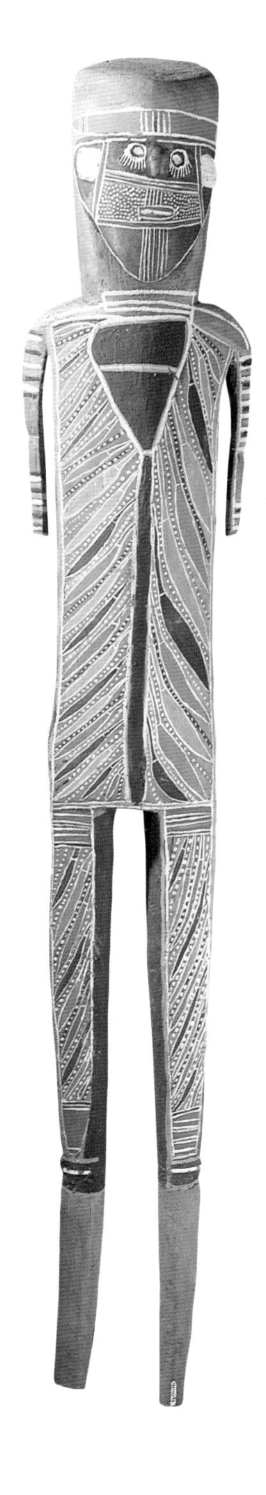

PLATE 55
Njinawanga
Maningrida/NT
Carving of bones 1982
Ochre, string, paper-bark, cotton fabric and wood
Various sizes
Rembarrnga Language Group
Balngara Clan

These innovative sculptures by Njinawanga depict violent death. The three carved wooden skulls and bones are those of a man and his two daughters. They were killed because the man refused to honour his promise to give the daughters in marriage. The sculptures are both historical and allegorical because they depict incidents said to have happened many years ago which illustrate the tragic results of failing to conform to social norms.

PLATE 56
Baluka Maymuru
Yirrkala/NT
Yingalpiya, the Milky Way crocodile 1987
Ochre on wood
179 x 18 x 18cm
Manggalili Clan
Yirritja Moiety

The Milky Way is a river in the night sky. It is called Milnguya, which is also the name of a river at Blue Mud Bay near Djarrakpi. This river is the nesting place for the freshwater crocodile, Yingalpiya. Here, long ago, the Ancestral Men – Munuminya and Yikuywanga – were fishing for guruka *(rock cod) in the river. Their canoe overturned and they drowned, despite the attempts of the crocodile to save them. The spirits of the men went up to the Milky Way. With them in the Milky Way are the crocodile, the bark canoe and the rock cod that they had caught before their canoe overturned. The many stars of the Milky Way are the spirits of the Manggalili people who have gone to join their ancestors.*

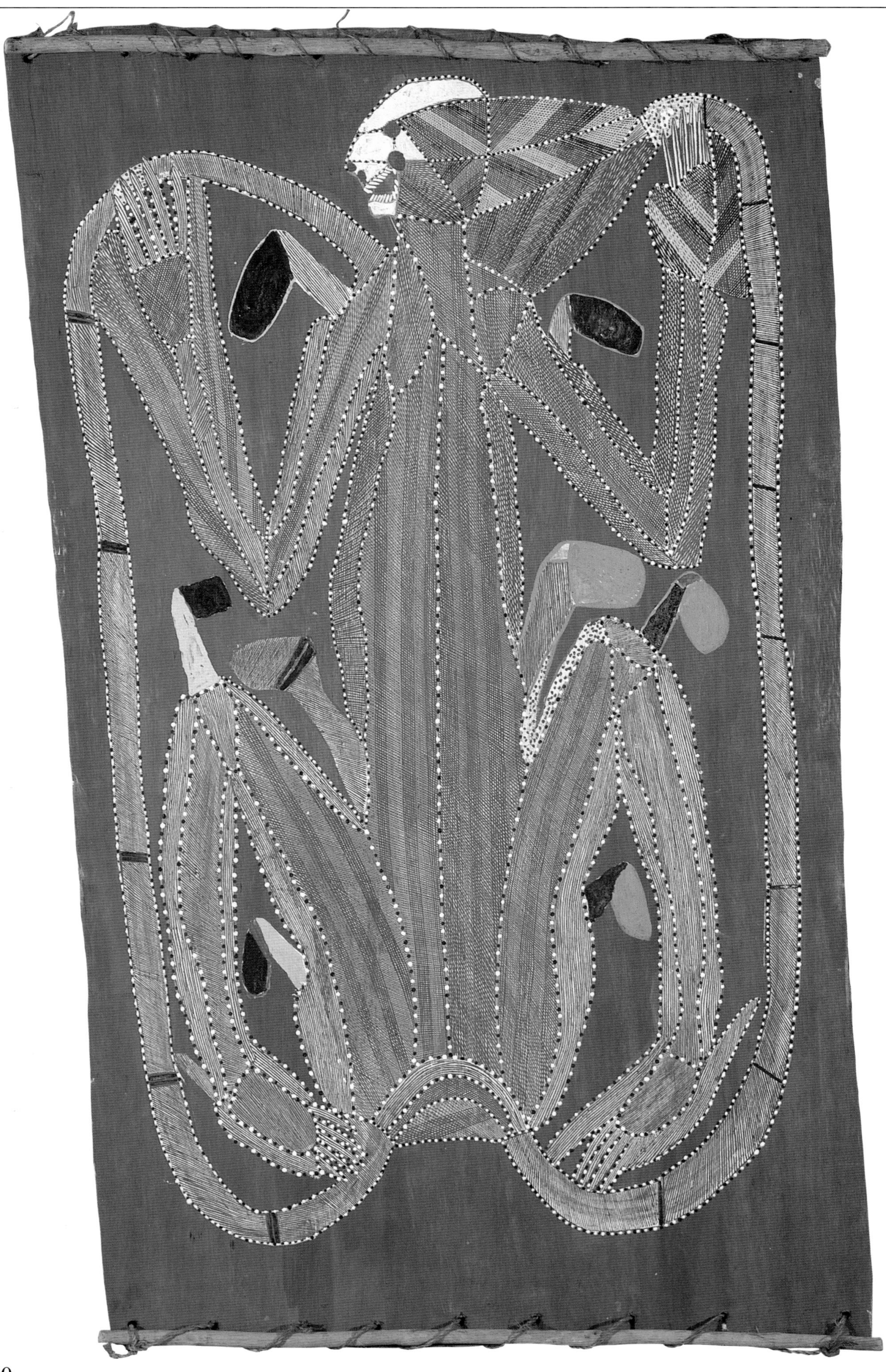

PLATE 57
Njiminjuma
Mormega/NT
Namarrgon, the lightning spirit 1981
Ochre on bark
88 x 55cm irreg
Kunwinjku Language Group
Nagurrulk Clan

Namarrgon, the Lightning Spirit, is an important Being from western Arnhem Land, who is associated with the thunder and lightning of the wet season. Namarrgon is always depicted with stone axes protruding from his joints. He uses these to strike the ground to make the thunder. He also has a circuit of power, indicative of lightning, which connects his head with his testicles. This power is emphasised by the protuberance from his head and shoulders.

PLATE 58
Peter Maralwanga (deceased)
Maragalidban/NT
Yawk Yawk spirit 1974
Ochre on bark
96.5 x 48cm irreg
Kunwinjku Language Group
Nagardbam Clan

Yawk Yawk is a female Spirit who is said to have grown a fish tail when she entered the water after a hunting trip. This particular Spirit lives in a deep rock pool in Malwon Creek, near Maningrida in central Arnhem Land.

PLATE 59
Curly Bardagubu (deceased)
Maningrida/NT
Moon spirit 1974
Ochre on bark
96 x 45.6cm irreg
Kunwinjku Language Group
Naborn Clan

The Moon Dreaming Spirit, Dird, who lives at a site called Namagadarbu, is depicted in this painting. He represents the bones of the moon when it dies or wanes, before it is later re-born as the full moon. At the foot of the figure the moon is depicted as a crescent as well as a sphere. The feathered strings attached to his head and hands represent stars.

PLATE 60
Peter Maralwanga (deceased)
Maragalidban/NT
Three spirits of the rock country 1980
Ochre on bark
139.5 x 52.5cm irreg
Kunwinjku Language Group
Nagardbam Clan

The Kunwinjku Language Group of central Arnhem Land have many stories about Spirit Beings who live amongst the rocks of the escarpment country. This painting depicts a family of mimi *spirits from the artist's country near the headwaters of the Cadell River. These are very shy, friendly spirits, which are very rarely seen by humans.*

PLATE 61
Jack Kaiwulan
Jaruluk/NT
Mimi spirits 1984
Bark, string and ochre on wood
108.1 x 16 x 12.1cm with base
85.2 x 10.2 x 10.1cm with base
Maiali Language Group

Mimi *spirits are said to live in a similar way to humans. They hunt and gather and observe the same rules of social behaviour. These two* mimi *figures are husband and wife – the woman is from the Ngarritjin subsection of the Yirritja moiety married to a Balang man of the Dhuwa moiety.*

PLATE 62
Curly Bardagubu (deceased)
Maningrida/NT
Kumoken – the crocodile 1976
Ochre on bark
129.5 x 115.2cm irreg
Kunwinjku Language Group
Naborn Clan

Back in the Dreamtime, Kumoken the salt water crocodile emerged from the earth, inland beyond the mountain ranges. As he made his way slowly to the sea, the trail he made with his tail slowly filled with water to become the Liverpool River.

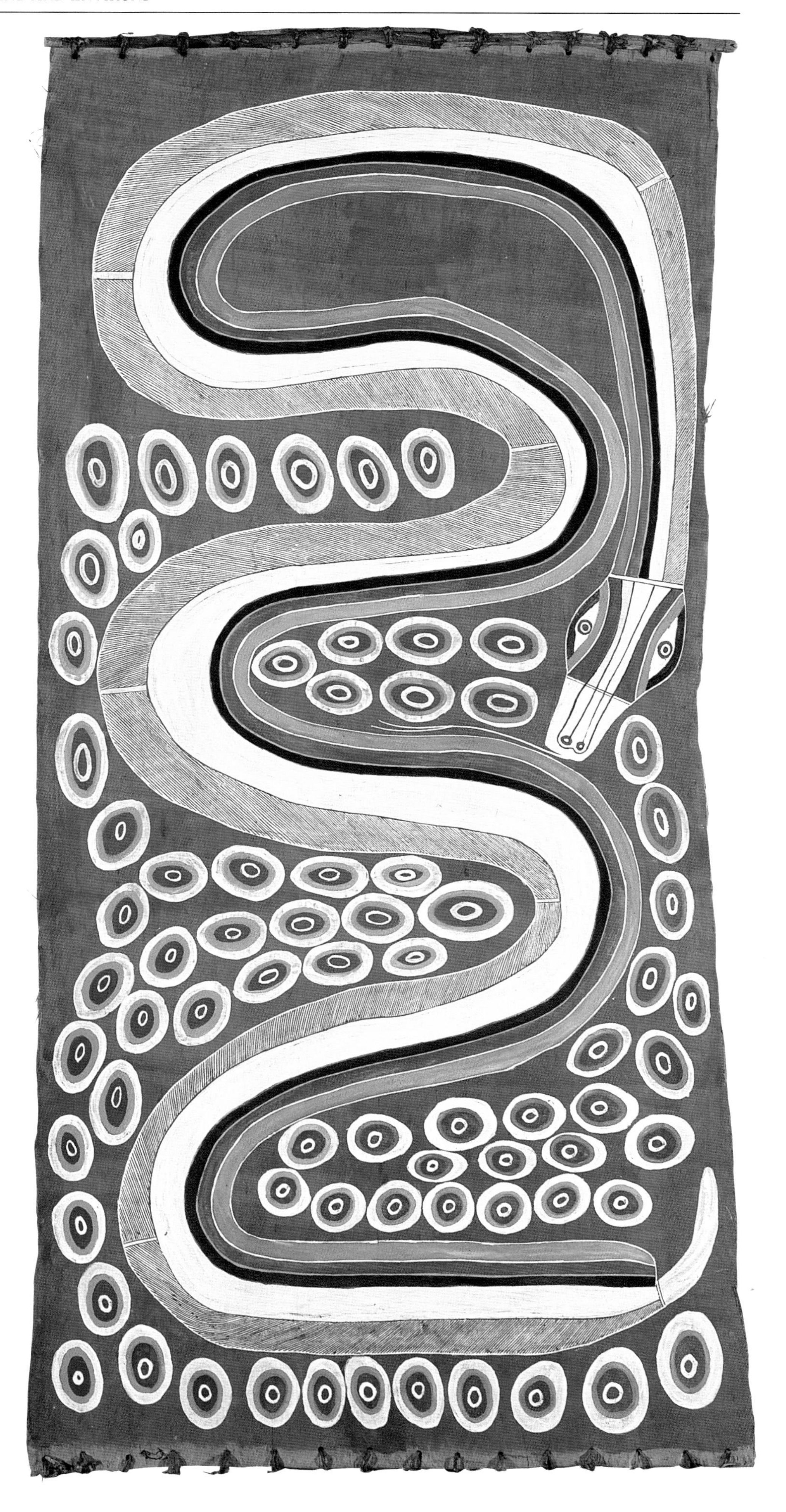

PLATE 63
Curly Bardagubu (deceased)
Maningrida/NT
Yingarna 1980
Ochre on bark
183.5 x 87.7cm irreg
Kunwinjku Language Group
Naborn Clan

Yingarna is the original and most powerful Rainbow Snake in western Arnhem Land. She is the originator of all Ancestral Beings and the clans associated with them. According to the version given by this artist, Yingarna was annoyed by the odd shapes, half animal-half human, that the creatures around her assumed. She swallowed them and regurgitated them in the shapes that they bear today. From her eggs she gave birth to Ngalyod, the other Rainbow Serpent, and a daughter, Ngalgunburijami.

These serpents are often depicted in the form of snakes. However they can also be depicted as hybrids, incorporating some of the characteristics of the totemic species associated with them.

PLATE 64
Djawida
Gudjekbinj/NT
Nawora, the dreamtime being 1985
Ochre on bark
178.5 x 53.5cm irreg
Kunwinjku Language Group
Yulkman Clan

Nawora is a Dreamtime Being who lives in the artist's stone country at Gudjekbinj (an outstation of Oenpelli) in Ngalngbali country. During the Dreamtime he travelled through this country with his wives who wore dillybags around their heads. Nawora has six toes and fingers and can transform himself into different shapes, such as a bird-man and the powerful Rainbow Serpent. In this painting he has the head of a bird. Nawora created certain sites as he travelled and taught Aboriginal women how to make dillybags and fishing nets from the inner bark of particular trees. One of his wives is carrying a fishing net as well as her dillybag (top left). The painting also illustrates some of the freshwater species which live in the waterholes of his country.

PLATE 65
Gubargu
Maningrida/NT
Ngalyod, the Rainbow Serpent 1980
Ochre on bark
117 x 100.5cm irreg
Kunwinjku Language Group
Nagulmaru Clan

In the centre of the Nagulmaru clan estate is a deep rock pool on the Mann River where Ngalyod, the Rainbow Serpent lives. The rock pool is depicted here as the two spaces between the twinning snakes. This gives a clear impression of the relative size of Ngalyod, who is considered a potentially dangerous and powerful Being, associated with the rain of the wet season and the related productivity of the land. If provoked, Ngalyod can cause severe storms and floods.

PLATE 66
Bangul and Mawalan (deceased)
Yirrkala/NT
Bremer Island turtle hunter
Ochre on bark
59 x 141cm irreg
Rirratjingu Clan
Dhuwa Moiety

This painting shows the Ancestral Turtle Hunter's two sons, Minjaba and Wulwul, returning to Dambalia after having speared a green turtle. In the other panel, the Green Turtle Woman, Waiaba, and the Turtle Man, Makban, are depicted in turtle form. Both can today be seen as rocks offshore. The black dividing line between the two panels refers to Mururuma's turtle stick, which has become a ritual emblem. The background is symbolic of seaweed and waves. (Mawalan was assisted by his daughter, Bangul, who did the fine in-fill work.)

PLATE 67
Dawudi (deceased)
Milingimbi/NT
Yulunggul emerging 1967
Ochre on bark
80.5 x 54cm irreg
Liyalawumirri Language Group
Galwanuk Clan
Dhuwa Moiety

The Ancestral Snake, Yulunggul is associated with the Wagilag Sisters. They are important Beings who introduced a number of rituals to the people of the Dhuwa moiety. Yulunggul is shown emerging from his waterhole in the centre of the painting. His wife forms the frame of the painting. She is depicted with her eggs, which are linked together like a chain. In the centre, his head takes on the shape of a sacred cabbage palm. Also depicted are a male and female goanna, two freshwater fish and some caterpillars.

PLATE 68
Djawa I (deceased)
Milingimbi/NT
Mangrove crabs 1978
Ochre on bark
118.5 x 49cm irreg
Gupapuyngu Language Group
Daygurrgurr Clan
Yirritja Moiety

The Djangkawu, the most important Ancestral Beings in north-eastern Arnhem Land, are believed to have been the original Ancestors of present day Aborigines. They belong to the Dhuwa moiety. This painting refers to a Djangkawu man and his two sisters, who are depicted at the base of the painting. It is a story about their travels on the mainland, opposite Elcho Island. Here they made freshwater wells and walked into the mangroves where they saw and named many fish and crabs. The mangrove crabs depicted here have a white decorative pattern which symbolises the foam on the water's surface.

PLATE 69
Yanggarriny
Yirrkala/NT
Barama story 1967
Ochre on bark
90.8 x 53.5cm irreg
Dhalwangu Clan
Yirritja Moiety

This relates to the journey of the great Yirritja Being, Barama, who after emerging from a waterhole at Gululdji, floated on a log down the river to Garngaran. This painting depicts the freshwater, long-necked tortoises which rested their heads on the log. The wavy lines and dots emanating from their feet are the weeds swaying in the water as they swim along. The dots are air bubbles. The horizontal dividing panel is the tree rangga *(sacred object) held by Barama. The other horizontal bands are logs washed into the river by floods. The birds are pied herons sitting on the river bank.*

PLATE 70
Nanyin
Yirrkala/NT
The myth of Ngulumung 1967
Ochre on bark
132.9 x 56cm irreg
Manggalili Clan
Yirritja Moiety

This painting relates to a sacred site in Blue Mud Bay, where the Ancestral Being Laindjung appointed Ngulumung, a mythical Ancestor of the Manggalili clan, as custodian of the sacred objects or rangga *for his people. Ngulumung is depicted holding these sacred* rangga *in his hands. The background design indicates running water, water weeds and air bubbles (dashes) in the foliage of the reeds. The top panel shows the Dreaming place of the Kingfish, Nuigal, who is another Being associated with the Manggalili clan. The bottom panel shows a design which is also associated with the Manggalili clan. According to this version, the central shape is a stone that was carried in the vagina of an Ancestral Woman and when it was removed, it went into a sacred well where it became a sacred* rangga. *It is associated with its constant companions Bildu, the snapper fish.*

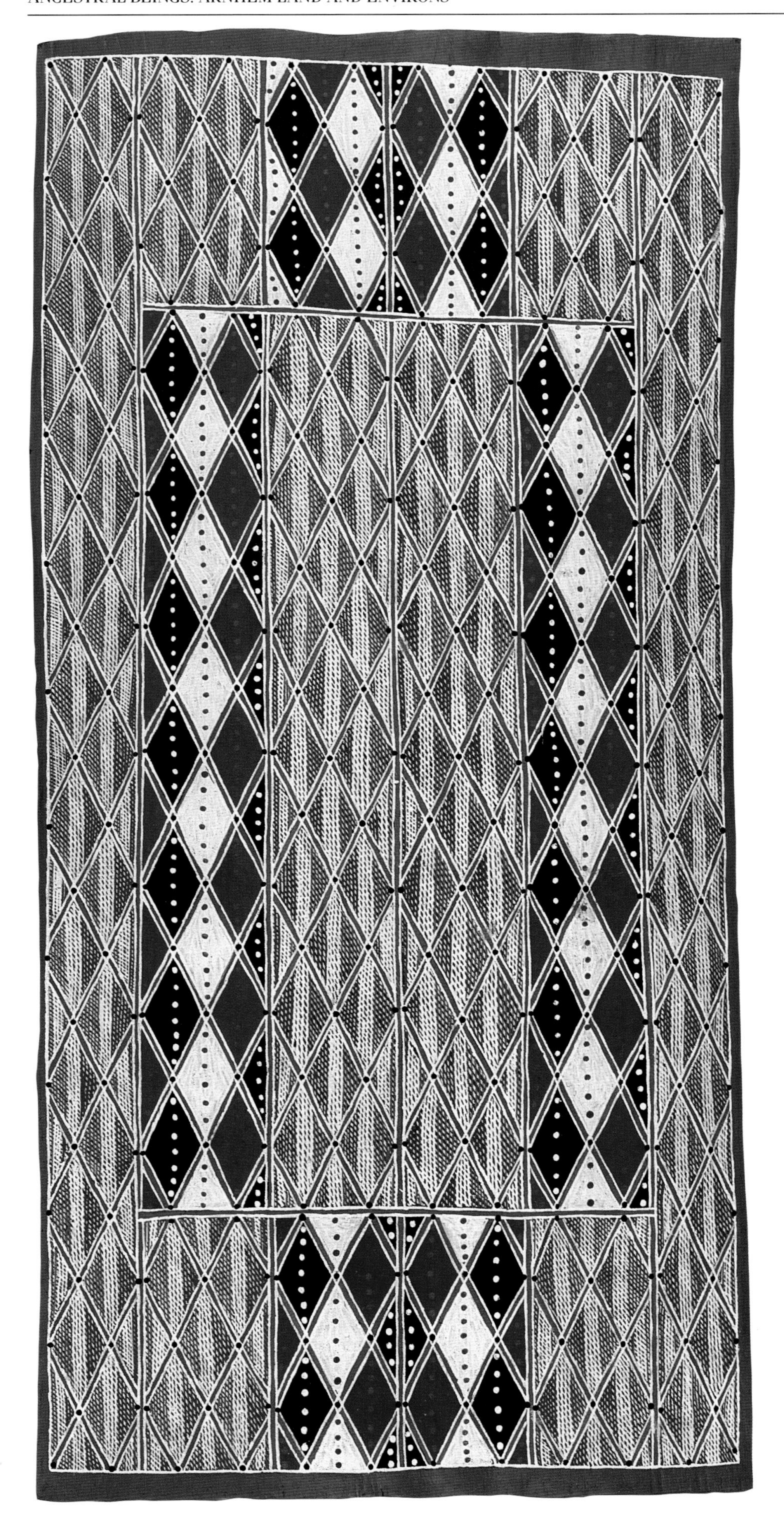

PLATE 71
Jimmy Wululu
Ramingining/NT b.1949
Honey clan design 1987
Ochre on bark
124.2 x 60cm irreg
Gupapuyngu Language Group
Daygurrgurr Clan
Yirritja Moiety

This is the primary totem for the artist and is associated with the Niwuda Honey story. The diamond pattern represents the honeycomb, or the cells of the native bee and the black diamonds indicate the empty cells. The white outlines of the cells indicate the beeswax and the dotted lines are the bees' larvae.

PLATE 72
George Milpurrurru
Ramingining/NT
Honey ancestor 1984
Ochre on bark
130 x 87.5cm irreg
Ganalbuyngu Language Group
Gurrumba Gurrumba Clan
Yirritja Moiety

Mewal,the Honey Ancestor and his wife are depicted as they travelled through the bush at Blue Mud Bay with their digging sticks, pandanus dillybags and other implements used for collecting honey from the sugarbag bees' hive. The cone shapes in the painting are Mewal's special dillybags, which are tightly woven to hold the honey. The oblong shapes, some of which are shown protruding from the dillybags, are Mewal's digging sticks. As Mewal and his wife journeyed they met the Crow Spirit and that of the Friar Bird. To get honey they cut trees down, and as the trees fell they created rivers. The frilly-lizard, the marbled gecko and the stinging caterpillar live in these trees and they are symbolised by the line patterns at the top of the painting. As Mewal travelled, he taught the people his laws and ceremonies and left a spiritual life force in the land wherever he camped.

PLATE 73
Mithinari (deceased)
Yirrkala/NT
The Djangkawu 1967
Ochre on bark
38 x 115.5cm irreg
Galpu Clan
Dhuwa Moiety

This bark depicts the sacred waterhole (in the centre) which the Djangkawu made for the Galpu clan. It is located in the flat coastal plain country which is covered with paperbarks (the background design). As they placed the sacred rangga *objects in it, the water rose up (horizontal band). Swamp birds on the lagoon are also depicted.*

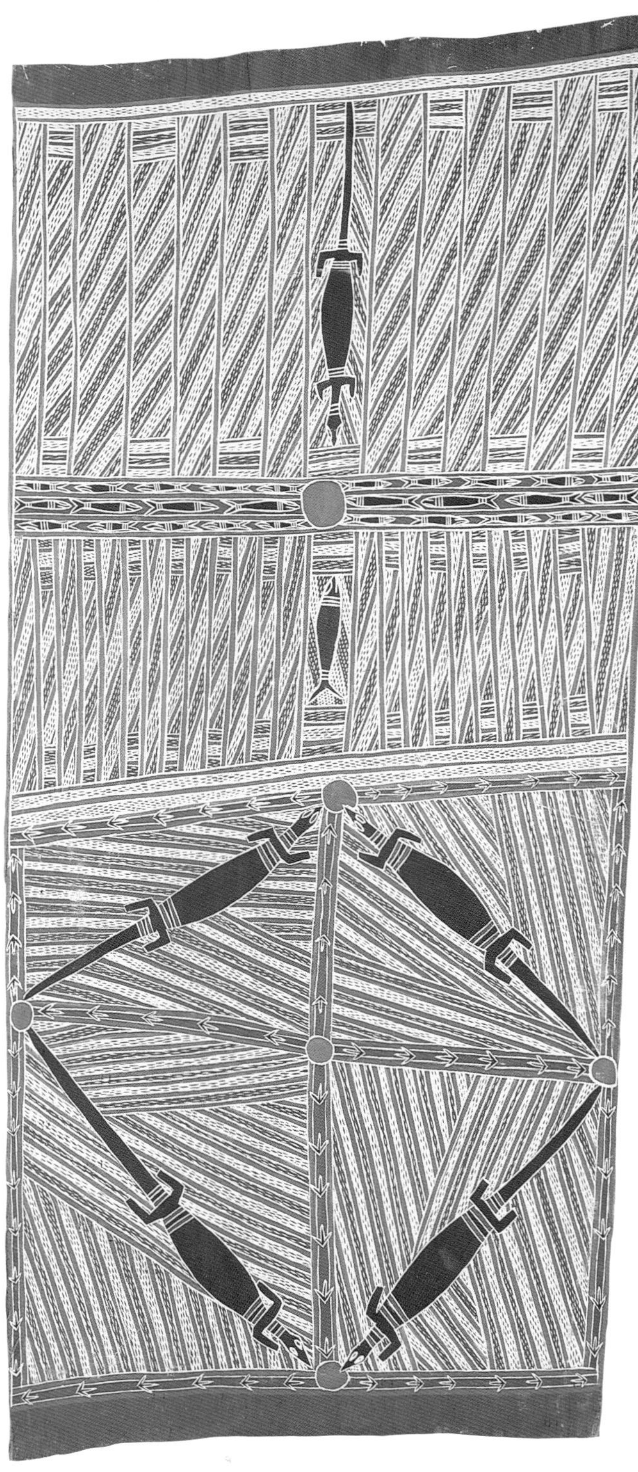

PLATE 74
Larrtjanga
Yirrkala/NT
Djangkawu story 1979
Ochre on bark
173 x 78cm irreg
Ngaymil Clan
Dhuwa Moiety

Journeys of the Djangkawu Ancestral Beings, in Ngaymil clan country, are referred to in this painting. As the Djangkawu travelled through the land they made sacred waterholes, represented by the circles in the painting. These central waterholes are at Miliba. Also depicted are the sand goanna and a skinny freshwater fish, as well as a number of smaller fish species, ngarganbal. *The background represents overflowing water covered with* dara *(wild banana) leaves. All these species were given to the Ngaymil people by the Djangkawu as good food. The lower panel shows* djanda *– goannas in the well at Dararwoi which is completely covered with wild banana leaves. The place derives its name from them and is situated south-east of the mouth of the Goromuru River in eastern Arnhem Land.*

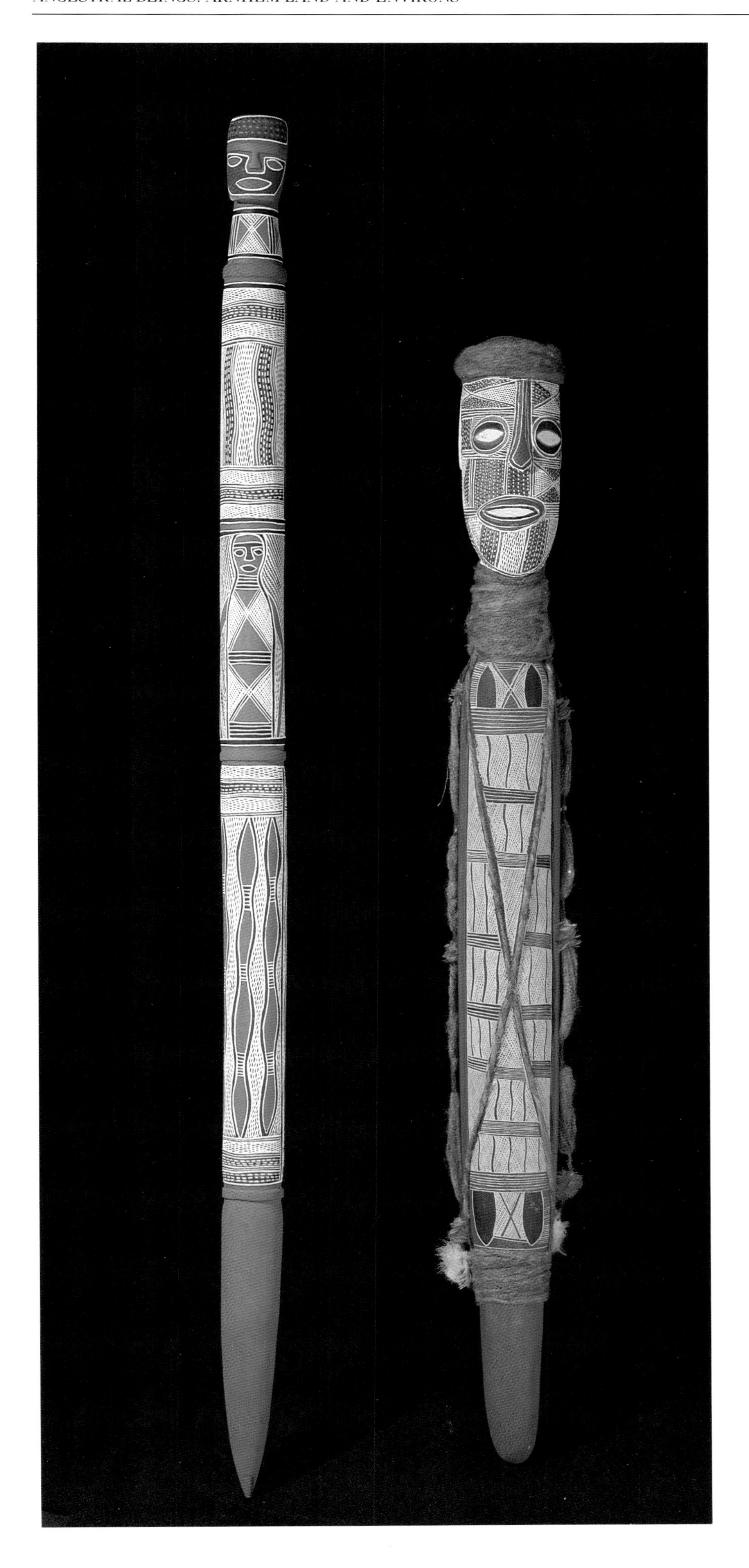

PLATE 75
Left
Banapana Maymuru (deceased)
Yirrkala/NT
Nyapililngu
Ochre on wood
175 x 7 x 9cm
Manggalili Clan
Yirritja Moiety

Right
Narritjin Maymuru (deceased)
Yirrkala/NT
Nyapililngu 1981
Feathers, possum fur and ochre
on wood
147 x 14 x 12cm
Manggalili Clan
Yirritja Moiety

The two carvings depict the Ancestral Being, Nyapililngu, with a digging stick torso. The digging stick is a sacred object associated with Nyapililngu. The shape of the digging stick also represents the salt water lake at Djarrakpi, where Nyapilingu made her camp.
These two carvings and the three bark paintings in the exhibition are a set that relate to the myth of the Ancestral Being, Nyapililngu who travelled west from Groote Eylandt to Djarrakpi at Cape Shield. She travelled with her digging stick and made her camp on the western sea-water side of the lake at Djarrakpi. With her digging stick, Nyapililngu created the salt water of the lake. On the opposite side of the lake were the Ancestral Beings, Guwak, the Nightbird and Marrngu, the Possum Ancestors, who made their camp in a marrawili *or cashew tree. The dew from a spider's web formed a cloud over the* marrawili *tree. The possums watched the spider in the tree spinning its web, and from this learnt to make possum-fur string which turned into the sand-dunes on their side of the lake. Nyapililngu copied them and her string became the dunes on her side of the lake. The possums then distributed lengths of possum-fur string to the other clans, but the largest lengths went to the Manggalili clan. Nyapililngu is said to be the progenitor of the Manggalili people, living today in north-eastern Arnhem Land. She also instigated social and ritual behaviour. For example, when Guwak died in the* marrawili *or cashew tree, Nyapililngu performed the first mortuary ceremony and taught the people the other procedures for a mortuary ritual.*

PLATE 76
Mick Numieri Tjapaltjarri
Papunya/NT
Goanna dreaming 1975
Synthetic polymer paint on
composition board
33.8 x 75.3cm irreg
Pintubi Language Group

This painting relates to the journey of some Ancestral Goanna Men through the arid Pintubi country. One of the Goannas is depicted in the centre, flanked on either side by the semi-circular camps made by the Goanna Men during their journey.

PLATE 77
Johnny Wararrngula Tjupurrula
Papunya/NT
Possum dreaming 1975
Synthetic polymer paint on composition board
128.8 x 45.5cm irreg
Luritja Language Group

A Possum Dreaming ceremony is referred to in this painting. The border represents the ceremony and the oval shapes are ceremonial shields used by the dancers. The Possum is symbolised by his footprints.

PLATE 78
Mick Numieri Tjapaltjarri
Papunya/NT
Death story 1972
Synthetic polymer paint
on composition board
51 x 35.4cm irreg
Pintubi Language Group

The ancient journey undertaken by a family through arid desert country is depicted in this painting. They were looking for waterholes (the circles) but as they were all dry, the family perished from thirst.

PLATE 79
Anatjari Tjakamarra
Papunya/NT
Ceremony 1974
Synthetic polymer paint
on composition board
67.3 x 38.4cm irreg
Pintubi Language Group

A men's ceremony is depicted in this painting. Because of its sacred nature the ceremony has no detailed explanation. In the centre, the spiral represents the body paint designs worn by the participants. The concentric circles depict a large ceremonial ground, and the 'U' shapes are the male performers. The oval shapes represent sacred objects which were brought out for viewing during the ritual. (Permission to exhibit this painting was obtained from the artist.)

PLATE 80
John Tjakamarra
Papunya/NT
Ceremonial camp 1972
Synthetic polymer paint
on composition board
56.2 x 56.8cm irreg
Pintubi Language Group

A ceremonial camp (represented by the circle) where uninitiated boys are waiting to be decorated, is depicted in this painting. No other details were given.

PLATE 81
Yala Yala Gibbs Tjungarrayi
Papunya/NT
Wiltja story 1972
Synthetic polymer paint
on composition board
50 x 37.2cm irreg
Pintubi Language Group

This relates to a myth concerning an old man who is left to die in a bush-shelter, wiltja. *Suddenly a gusty wind came from the north-west and blew the shelter into the sky. The lines in the painting depict the pieces of the shelter.*

PLATE 82
Johnny Wararrngula Tjupurrula
Papunya/NT
Water dreaming 1975
Synthetic polymer paint
on composition board
51 x 50.5cm irreg
Luritja Language Group

This painting is associated with a rain-making ceremony. Ceremonial objects used in the ritual are shown between the wavy lines of the water. The water flows into the circular waterholes. The parallel lines indicate the growth of plants after the rain fall. The figure is the Spirit of death through starvation – the spectre of what can happen if the rain ceremony is unsuccessful.

PLATE 83
Shorty Lungkata Tjungarrayi
Papunya/NT
Rat kangaroo dreaming
1972
Synthetic polymer paint
on composition board
62 x 66cm irreg
Pintubi Language Group

The central square represents the camp of the Ancestral Rat Kangaroo. The other squares represent the caves surrounding his camp.

PLATE 78

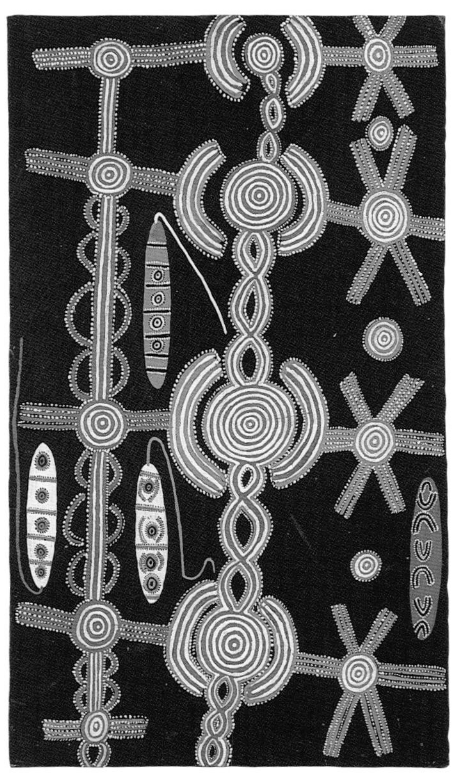

PLATE 79

PLATE 80

PLATE 82

PLATE 81

PLATE 83

PLATE 84
Uta Uta Tjangala
Kintore/NT
Kuma, snake dreaming 1982
Synthetic polymer paint on canvas
181.3 x 74.5cm
Pintubi Language Group

Relating to two men who, in mythological times, helped the Kuma or Snake, the painting's story is a Men's Dreaming and is associated with the site of tubalinya. The men, one of the tjangala kinship subsection and the other a Tjungurrayi subsection, followed the Snake and helped him on his way east.

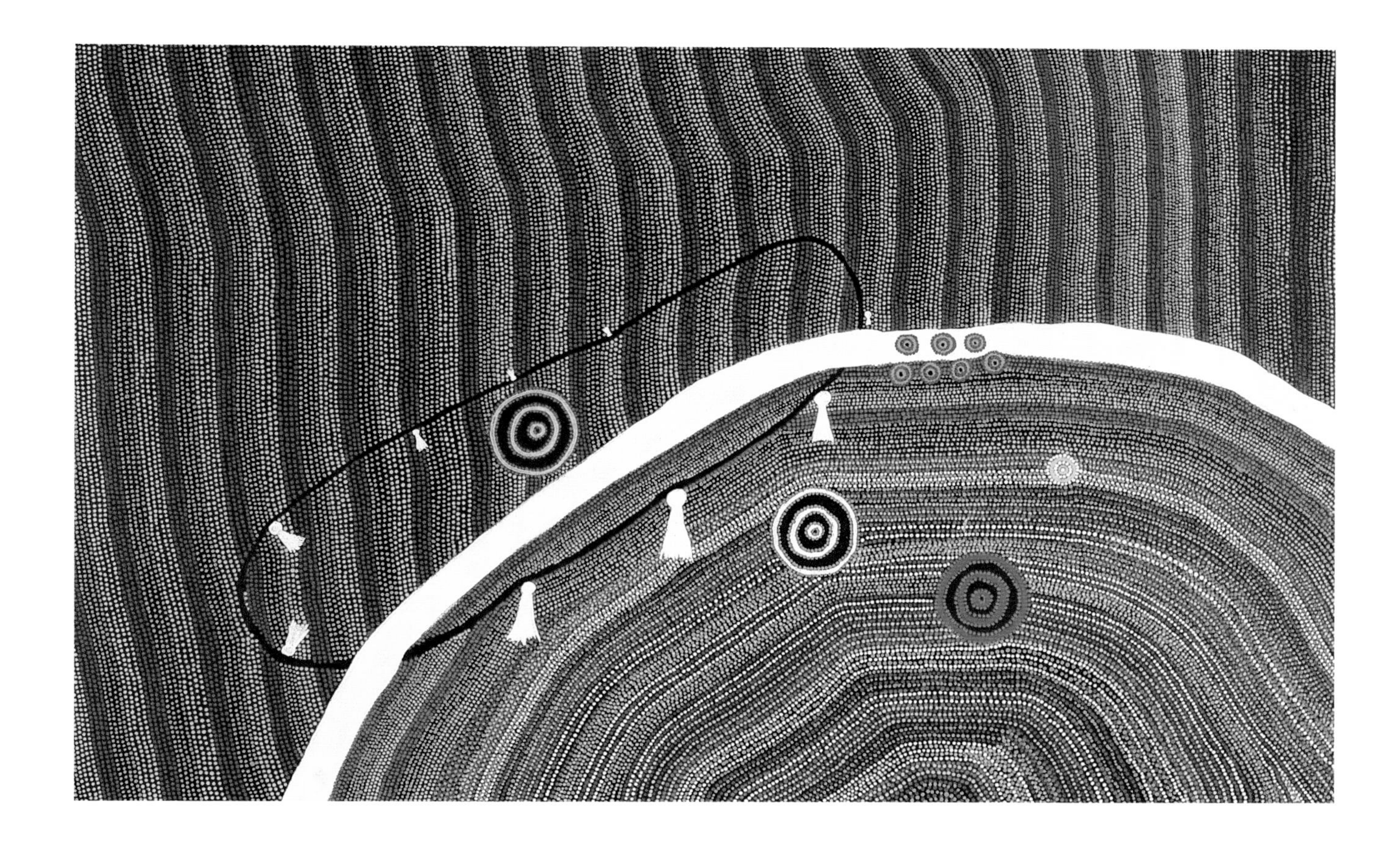

PLATE 85
Bronson Nelson Tjakamarra
Yuendumu/NT
Halley's Comet 1986
Synthetic polymer paint on canvas
78 x 126cm
Warlpiri Language Group

This painting is an interesting example of the innovations occurring in the work of some contemporary Aboriginal artists. The artist was inspired by a technical drawing in a magazine showing the trajectory of Halley's Comet. He has used this as the main element of the design. The path of the comet is shown as a loop, with the comet at various stages of its orbit circling the sun. The other planets depicted as circles are the Earth, the Moon, the Pleiades (the group of circles) and Venus – (the Morning Star). The white band bisecting the picture is the Milky Way and the dots represent the stars. Although the Warlpiri people have a generic name for a comet – warnawara *– there is no specific mythology attached to them. The Milky Way and the Pleiades, or the Seven Sisters are included in this painting because they are important Dreamings.*

PLATE 86
Billy Stockman Tjapaltjarri
Papunya/NT
Men's dreaming 1980
Synthetic polymer paint on canvas
168 x 337.5cm
Anmatyerre Language Group

This painting depicts the journey of two men – one of the Tjungurrayi subsection group and one of the Tjapaltjarri subsection group – who travelled to Mt Dennison during the Dreamtime. On the way they performed ceremonies. The sinuous line and the footprints indicate the path of their journey. The circles at either end represent their camp at Mt Dennison. The 'U' shapes are Tjungurrayi and Tjapaltjarri sitting down. The other circles flanked by parallel lines illustrate the body designs they wore during ceremonies.

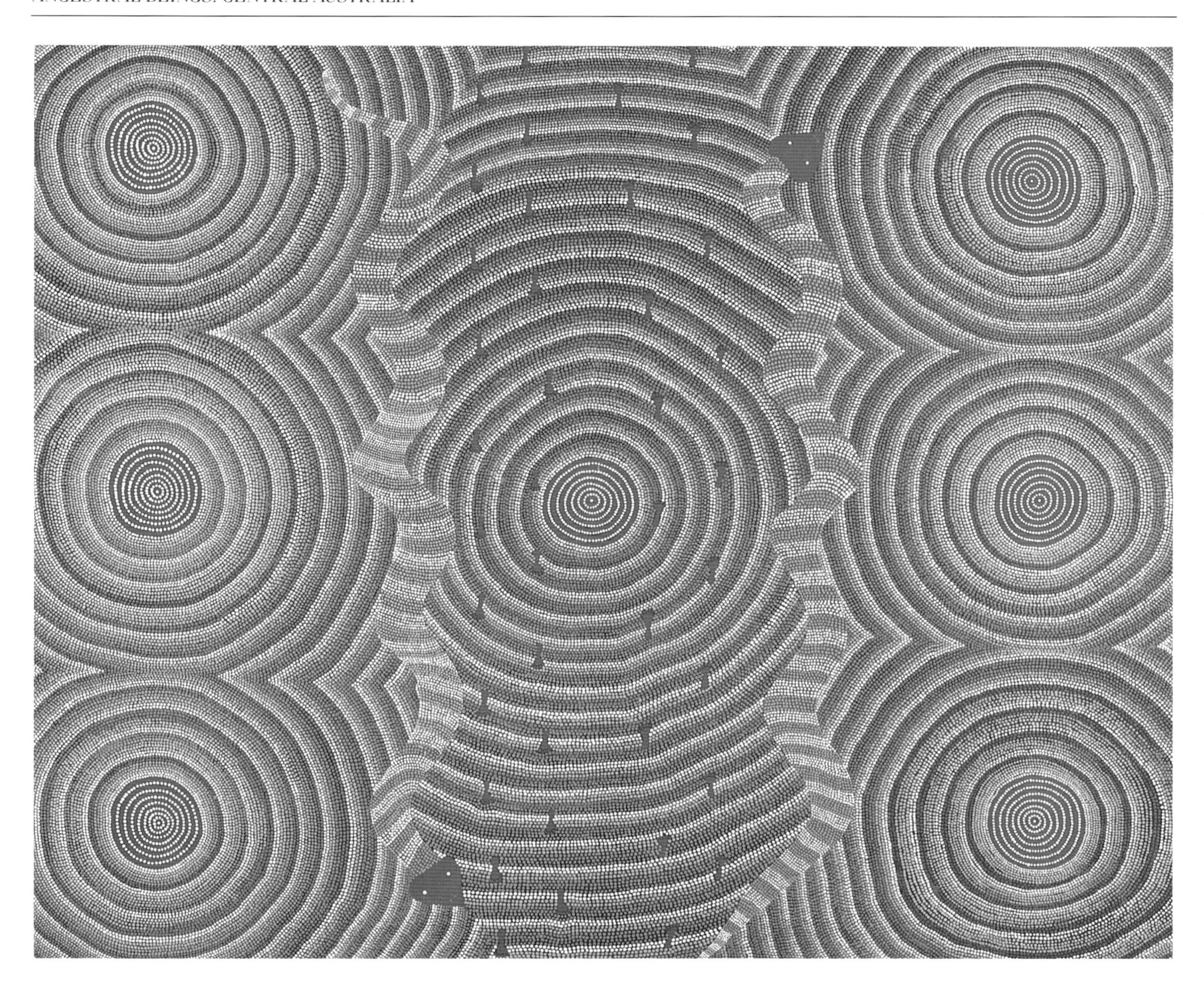

PLATE 87
Riley Major Tjangala
Papunya/NT
Snake dreaming 1987
Synthetic polymer paint on canvas
151.2 x 181.3cm
Pintubi Language Group

The design of this painting is associated with the Snake Dreaming site at Kakarra, to the east of Kintore community near the Northern Territory and Western Australian border. The Snake Man of the Tjakamarra subsection group and his wife lived at this site. They are represented by both the snakes and the footprints. The circles are the sand-hills at Kakarra. According to legend, the cutting between these sand-hills occurred during the Dreamtime, when the Snake travelled between them.

Namatjira and the Hermannsburg School

PLATE 88
Albert Namatjira
Hermannsburg/NT
Mount Ormiston, McDonald Ranges
c. early 1940s
Watercolour on wove paper
26.4 x 36.5cm
Arrernte (Aranda) Language Group

The Arrernte (Aranda) artist, Albert Namatjira was the first Aborigine to receive acclaim for excelling in a European mode of painting. Born at Hermannsburg Lutheran Mission in central Australia in 1902, Namatjira was 33 when he received his first instruction in watercolour landscape painting from the visiting artist Rex Battarbee. Namatjira rapidly mastered this new technique and from his first one-man exhibition in 1938 until his death in 1959, he received so much acclaim that he became arguably one of Australia's most famous artists.

Namatjira's sons and close relatives also began to paint and to develop their own personalised

PLATE 89
Athanasius Renkaraka
Hermannsburg/NT
Hermannsburg settlement
c. early 1960s
Watercolour on wove paper
50 x 70.7cm
Arrernte (Aranda)
Language Group

interpretations of the landscape. While their art was based upon the European tradition of classical landscape painting, it also became an important vehicle for expressing the artists' relationship to their tribal land with its myriad of religious sites. Because of this fusion of ideas, the Hermannsburg School was the first significant transitional art movement to emerge from traditional Aboriginal Australia.

PLATE 90
Albert Namatjira
Hermannsburg/NT
Ghost gum c. 1940s
Watercolour on wove paper
36.6 x 25cm
Arrernte (Aranda) Language Group

PLATE 91
Edwin Pareroultja
Hermannsburg/NT
Untitled landscape c.early 1960s
Watercolour on wove paper
34.5 x 26.5cm
Arrernte (Aranda) Language Group

PLATE 92
Kenneth Entata
Hermannsburg/NT
Untitled landscape c. early 1960s
Watercolour on wove paper
23 x 71.3cm
Arrernte (Aranda) Language Group

PLATE 93
Otto Pareroultja
Hermannsburg/NT
Untitled landscape c. early 1960s
Watercolour on wove paper
37 x 55.2cm
Arrernte (Aranda) Language Group

PLATE 94
Gabriel Namatjira
Hermannsburg/NT
Untitled landscape c. early 1960s
Watercolour on wove paper
24.2 x 34cm
Arrernte (Aranda) Language Group

PLATE 95
Wenton Rubuntja
Hermannsburg/NT
Ingkwepeye-Tyinye 1985
Watercolour on wove paper
52.4 x 73.2cm
Arrernte (Aranda) Language Group

Bibliography

Rock art of the Northern Terrritory

Brandl, E. *Australian Aboriginal Paintings in Western and Central Arnhem Land.* Australian Institute of Aboriginal Studies, Canberra, 1973.

Chaloupka, G. *From Palaeoart to Casual Paintings: the chronological sequence of Arnhem Land Plateau rock art.* Monograph Series, No. 1, Northern Territory Museum of Arts and Sciences, Darwin, 1984.

Edwards, R. *The Art of the Alligator Rivers Region* (Alligator Rivers Region Environmental Fact Finding Study). Australian Government Printing Service, Canberra, 1974.

Flinders, M. *A Voyage to Terra Australis...* G. & W. Nicol, London, 1814.

Contemporary Aboriginal interpretations of western Arnhem Land rock paintings

Australia National Parks and Wildlife Service. *Kakadu National Park Plan of Management.* Australian Government Printing Service, Canberra, 1986.

Chaloupka, G. 'Chronological sequence of Arnhem Land Plateau rock art,' in R. Jones (ed.), *Archaeological Research in Kakadu National Park.* Australian National Parks and Wildlife Service Special Publication 13, 1985, pp. 269-280.

Chaloupka, *G. From Palaeoart to Casual Paintings: the chronological sequence of Arnhem Land Plateau rock art.* Monograph Series No. 1, Northern Territory Museum of Arts and Sciences, Darwin, 1984.

Chaloupka, G. 'Kakadu rock art: its cultural, historic and prehistoric significance,' in D. Gillespie (ed.), *The Rock Art Sites of Kakadu National Park: some preliminary research findings for their conservation and management.* Australian National Parks and Wildlife Service Special Publication No. 10, 1983, pp. 3-33.

Forge, A. 'Art and environment in the Sepik,' in Carol F. Jopling (ed.), *Art and Aesthetics in Primitive Societies.* E.P. Dutton, 1971, pp. 290-314.

Haskovec, I.P. and Sullivan, H. 'Najombolmi: reflections and rejections of an Aboriginal artist,' (1987) in Howard Morphy (ed.), *Animals into Art.* Allen and Unwin, (in press).

Jones, R. (ed.). *Archaeological Research in Kakadu National Park.* Australian National Parks and Wildlife Service Special Publication 13, 1985.

Jones, R. and Johnson, I. 'Deaf Adder Gorge: Lindner site, Nauwalabila 1,' in R. Jones (ed.), *Archaeological Research in Kakadu National Park.* Australian National Parks and Wildlife Service Special Publication 13, 1985, pp. 165-227.

Keen, I. 'The Alligator Rivers Aborigines – retrospect and prospect,' in R. Jones (ed.), *Northern Australia: options and implications.* Australian National University, Canberra, 1980, pp. 171-186.

Schrire, C. 'The Alligator Rivers: prehistory and ecology in western Arnhem Land,' *Terra Australis* 6. Australian National University, Canberra, 1982.

Taçon, P.S.C. 'Art and the essence of being: symbolic and economic aspects of fish among the peoples of Western Arnhem Land, Australia,' (1987a) in Howard Morphy (ed.), *Animals into Art.* Allen and Unwin, (in press).

Taçon, P.S.C. Field journals, tapes and notebooks: field research in Kakadu National Park and Arnhem Land (1986), April 24, 1986 – January 29, 1987. Unpublished and lodged at the Australian National University, Canberra.

Taçon, P.S.C. 'Internal – external: a re-evaluation of the x-ray concept in Western Arnhem Land rock art,' *Rock Art Research* 4(1), 1987b, pp. 36-50.

New life for the Dreaming

Berndt, R.M. and C.H. *Man, Land and Myth in North Australia: The Gunwinggu People.* Ure Smith, 1970.

Brandl, E.J. *Australian Aboriginal Paintings in Western and Central Arnhem Land.* Australian Institute of Aboriginal Studies, Canberra, 1973.

Carroll, P.J. 'Mimi from western Arnhem Land,' in P.J. Ucko (ed.), *Form in Indigenous Art.* Australian Institute of Aboriginal Studies, Canberra, 1977, pp. 119-230.

Art and religion in eastern Arnhem Land

Morphy, H. 'Now you understand,' in N. Peterson and M. Langton (eds.), *Aborigines, Land and Landrights.* Australian Institute of Aboriginal Studies, Canberra, 1983.

Morphy, H. *Journey to the Crocodiles Nest.* Australian Institute of Aboriginal Studies, Canberra, 1984.

Groger-Wurm, H. *Australian Aboriginal Bark Paintings and their Mythological Interpretation.* Australian Institute of Aboriginal Studies, Canberra, 1973.

Women's acrylic paintings from Yuendumu

Forge, A. 'Schematisation and Meaning,' in P.J. Ucko (ed.), *Form in Indigenous Art.* Australian Institute of Aboriginal Studies, Canberra, 1977, pp. 28-32.

Levi-Strauss, C. *Structural Anthropology* 2. Peregrine Books, 1973.

Munn, N.D. *Walbiri Iconography: Graphic Representation and Cultural Symbolism in a Central Australian Society.* Cornell University Press, 1973.

Scoditti, G.M.G. 'Aesthetics: The significance of apprenticeship on Kitawa,' *Man* 17, 1982, pp. 74-91.

'Make 'im flash poor bugger'

Bardon, G. *Aboriginal Art of the Western Desert.* Rigby, Adelaide, 1979.

Brody, A. *The Face of the Centre: Papunya Tula Paintings 1971-84.* National Gallery of Victoria, Melbourne, 1985, (Catalogue).

Crocker, A. (ed.). *Papunya: Aboriginal Paintings from the Central Australian Desert.* Aboriginal Artists Agency and Papunya Tula Artists, Sydney, 1983. (Previously published as *Mr Sandman Bring Me a Dream,* 1981)

Isaacs, J. *Arts of the Dreaming: Australia's Heritage.* Lansdowne Press, Sydney, 1984.

Kimber, R. 'Central Australian and Western Desert Art: Some Impressions,' (1980) in Crocker, 1983, pp.7-9.

Maughan, J. and Zimmer, J. (eds.). *Dot and Circle: A Retrospective Survey of the Aboriginal Acrylic Paintings of Central Australia.* RMIT, Melbourne, 1986, (Catalogue).

Munn, N.D. *Walbiri Iconography. Graphic Representations and Cultural Symbolism in a Central Australian Society.* Cornell University Press, Ithaca, 1973.

Tjampitjinpa, Dinny Nolan. *Tjakulpa Kuwarritja.* Papunya Literature Production Centre, (in press).

Tjupurrula, Johnny Wararrngula. *Mala Tjukurrpa.* Papunya Literature Production Centre, (in press).

The economic basis for cultural reproduction

Altman, J.C. 'The structure and future of artefact manufacture for market exchange in north-central Arnhem Land,' in P. Loveday and P. Cooke (eds.), *Aboriginal Art and Craft and the Market.* North Australia Research Unit, Darwin, 1983.

Altman, J.C. *Hunter-Gatherers Today: An Aboriginal Economy in North Australia.* Australian Institute of Aboriginal Studies, Canberra, 1987.

Blanchard, C.A. (Chairman). *Return to Country: The Aboriginal Homelands Movement in Australia.* Australian Government Publishing Service, Canberra, 1987.

Harris, Kerr, Forster and Company. *Australia's Travel and Tourist Industry.* Harris, Kerr, Forster and Co. Publishers, Sydney, 1965.

Miller, M. (Chairman). *The Report of the Committee of Review of Aboriginal Employment and Training Programs.* Australian Government Printing Service, Canberra, 1985.

Northern Territory Development Corporation and Northern Territory Tourist Commission. *Initiatives for Tourist Facilities.* N.T.D.C. and N.T.T.C., Darwin, 1984.

Northern Territory Tourist Commission. *People of Two Times – The Aborigines of Australia's Northern Territory.* Northern Territory Tourist Commission, Darwin, 1987.

Profile of contributors

Dr Jon Altman

Dr Jon Altman has an academic background in economics and social anthropology. Most of Dr Altman's research has been on economic and cultural continuity and change at remote Aboriginal communities in northern Australia. His interest in the economics of the Aboriginal arts and crafts industry is closely linked to this research. Dr Altman is currently a Research Fellow at the Department of Political and Social Change, Research School of Pacific Studies, the Australian National University, Canberra.

George Chaloupka

George Chaloupka is a field anthropologist with the Museums and Art Galleries of the Northern Territory, Darwin. For the past twenty years he has been recording the extensive rock art galleries predominantly in the northern part of the Territory, as well as in the Centre and the Kimberleys. During this time he has recorded around 2,000 art sites.

Françoise Dussart

Françoise Dussart is a French post-graduate student at the Australian National University, Canberra. Born in Paris and raised in French Guinea, she received her Masters from the Sorbonne University, Paris. After two years of fieldwork in the Northern Territory, she is now completing her doctoral work on the aesthetics and ritual life of the Warlpiri people. Miss Dussart is also working on Aboriginal art exhibitions that will tour Europe and the United States.

Ian Green

Ian Green is a linguist currently completing his PhD at the Australian National University in Canberra on the Marrithiyel language. For this he has undertaken three years research in the Daly River region. He is presently employed by the Northern Territory Education Department, to develop the Pintupi/Luritja bilingual language programme at Papunya. During his four years at Papunya he has worked in close association with many of the Papunya Tula artists, recording their dialects and documenting information about the land and the Dreaming associations represented in artists' paintings.

Dr Howard Morphy

Dr Howard Morphy is an anthropologist whose research has concentrated on analysing the meaning of Aboriginal artistic systems, particularly in Arnhem Land. He has published extensively on Aboriginal art and was one of the main organisers of the Aboriginal Australia exhibition in 1981 and the Australian Institute of Aboriginal Studies conference 'Aboriginal Arts in Contemporary Australia' in 1984. Dr Morphy is currently employed at the Pitt Rivers Museum, Department of Ethnology and Prehistory, University of Oxford, England; previously he was a senior lecturer in anthropology at the Australian National University, Canberra.

Paul Taçon

Paul Taçon is an anthropology graduate from Trent University, Ontario, Canada. He has conducted anthropological and archaeological research in the north-west Territories and in northern and southern Ontario, Canada, in south Dakota in the United States of America and in the Cape York Peninsula and Gurig National Park in Australia. He is currently enrolled in a PhD in Anthropology and Prehistory at the Australian National University in Canberra and for this has conducted 16 months research on contemporary Aboriginal rock art and its significance in the Kakadu National Park in western Arnhem Land.

Dr Luke Taylor

Dr Luke Taylor is a Visiting Research Fellow at the Australian Institute of Aboriginal Studies, Canberra. He is currently working on the Institute's computerised Index of Aboriginal Visual Artists. This project is designed to help the market for Aboriginal art and craft by collecting biographical information on Aboriginal artists. Recently Luke has completed a doctoral thesis on the bark paintings of the western Arnhem Land region. This thesis is based on material gained during an extended period of field research with Kunwinjku language-speaking artists. Luke has also completed research on the central Australian graphic art system and recorded rock art in New South Wales, central Queensland and Cape York.

Margie West

Margie West is a graduate from the University of Queensland whose background is in art, museology and anthropology. She is currently employed by the Museums and Art Galleries of the Northern Territory in Darwin where she has concentrated on the Aboriginal art of the region with a special interest in the contemporary art and craft of the Tiwi on Bathurst Island. She has been responsible for putting together ethnographic displays and selling exhibitions of Aboriginal art at the Museum. She is also the founder and co-ordinator of the National Aboriginal Art Award, staged annually in Darwin.